# INTRODUCTION

THE BRITISH MUSEUM is approaching the 250th anniversary of its foundation. Its principal aims today are to be at the centre of international scholarship and to disseminate knowledge for the education, in the widest sense of the word, of all. This is achieved through display at the British Museum, and elsewhere by loans, a vigorous programme of lectures and seminars, and publication in large numbers of articles and books. From its earliest days in the eighteenth century, the Museum collected, displayed, stored and preserved the works of mankind (and, at that time, the works of nature too) with great earnestness. This was the Age of Enlightenment, and as the author of the first Museum guide wrote in 1761, 'Curiosity almost universally prevails . . . Nothing can conduce more to preserve the Learning which this latter Age abounds with, than having Repositories in every Nation to contain its Antiquities, such as is the Museum of Britain.'

ABOVE
*Sir Hans Sloane (1660–1753).*
*His collections constituted the foundation*
*of the British Museum in 1753.*
*Engraving by I. Faber, 1728.*

The British Museum has never simply been a museum of antiquities of Britain. In fact, for its first century of existence, rather little of British origin was collected. From the very beginning interests were universal, and though fashions in collecting can be detected over the years, the collection as it exists today must be the most balanced, in terms of world cultures and chronology, that exists anywhere. The collections are vast. For many of its temporary exhibitions, the British Museum does not need to borrow; it can simply dip into its remarkable reserves to treat subjects as diverse as Gold from South America, the Culture of the Maldives, Rembrandt Drawings and Hindu Religion.

The founding collection was formed by Sir Hans Sloane, a physician by profession and an antiquarian by inclination. Born in 1660, Sloane was, from the first, devoted to scientific enquiry. After a spell in the West Indies, he wrote a book on the natural history of Jamaica.

LEFT
*Montagu House, the*
*first home of the*
*British Museum.*

BELOW
*Stuffed giraffes on the*
*staircase of the old museum*
*in Montagu House.*

On his return to London he became a fashion-able doctor, which helped to finance his collecting activities.

On Sloane's death in 1753, his collection was counted as containing 79,575 objects, and this did not include the plant specimens in his herbarium and his library of books and manuscripts. Sloane had wanted his collection to be given to King George II for the nation. It was eventually transferred to Parliament after a public lottery raised money for the establishment of the Museum. A late-seventeenth-century mansion on the edge of London, Montagu House, was purchased for the purpose by the Board of Trustees, the chairman of which was, by virtue of his office, the Archbishop of Canterbury. The British Museum first opened its doors to the public on 15 January 1759, for 'studious and curious Persons' as they were described. There was no admission fee but a ticket had to be obtained by somewhat tortuous means and, once inside, it was necessary to join a guided tour.

ABOVE

*The Portland Vase, as famous for its chequered history as for its superb craftsmanship. Roman, early first century AD.*

The new museum started to collect enthusiastically, a large proportion of the acquisitions being donated. There was a bias towards natural history specimens in the earliest days, including material collected by Captain Cook on his circumnavigations of the world. Ethnographic objects also came from this source. Great Britain was active in voyages of discovery at this time but Britons were also discovering the classical world on the Grand Tour. Sir William Hamilton, British Envoy in Naples, collected Greek pottery and sent two boatloads to England (though only one of them arrived). It was through Hamilton that the Portland Vase eventually reached the British Museum. Charles Townley's celebrated collection of sculpture, amassed in Rome, was sold to the Museum. The defeat of Napoleon's army in Egypt led to the acquisition of the Rosetta Stone and other Egyptian antiquities. In 1816 came perhaps the greatest of all groups of sculptures which would be

LEFT

*Charles Townley (1737–1805) and his collection. Painting by Johan Zoffany.*

added to the collections: the fine marbles from the Parthenon in Athens. Lord Elgin had been appointed Ambassador at Constantinople in 1799. Concerned about the destruction of classical remains in Greece, he assembled a team of artists and architects to record what survived and later obtained permission from the authorities to remove carved stone. The sculptures arrived in London in 1802 and Elgin displayed them to the public. In financial difficulty, he sold them to the government fourteen years later, and when established in the Museum, they immediately created great interest.

British envoys and ambassadors played a significant part in adding to the archaeological collections. In Egypt the Consul General, Henry Salt, with the help of an agent, Giovanni Belzoni, formed a large collection that included much colossal sculpture such as the head of pharaoh Amenhotep III, purchased by the Museum Trustees in 1823. He also donated in 1818 the famous head of Ramesses II, the inspiration for Shelley's

*Moving the colossal head of Ramesses II to the new Egyptian Sculpture Gallery in 1834.*

'Ozymandias'. Fascination with the archaeology of the biblical lands spread collecting activities further to the Middle East. Claudius Rich, resident in Baghdad from 1811 to 1820, formed a small collection of inscribed bricks, cylinder seals and engraved tablets from the plains of the Rivers Tigris and Euphrates and in so doing laid the foundation of the Museum's collection of Babylonian and Assyrian antiquities.

By early in the nineteenth century it was becoming clear that Montagu House was too small for its task. Not only were the antiquities' collections growing rapidly but the natural history specimens and library were adding to the problem. Additionally there were pressures from the public who were coming in increasing numbers; in 1814 the Trustees pointed out that between 28,000 and 30,000 persons had visited the collections in the past year. The problem came to a head in 1823 when King George IV offered his father's library of nearly 85,000 items to the Museum. A year later it was

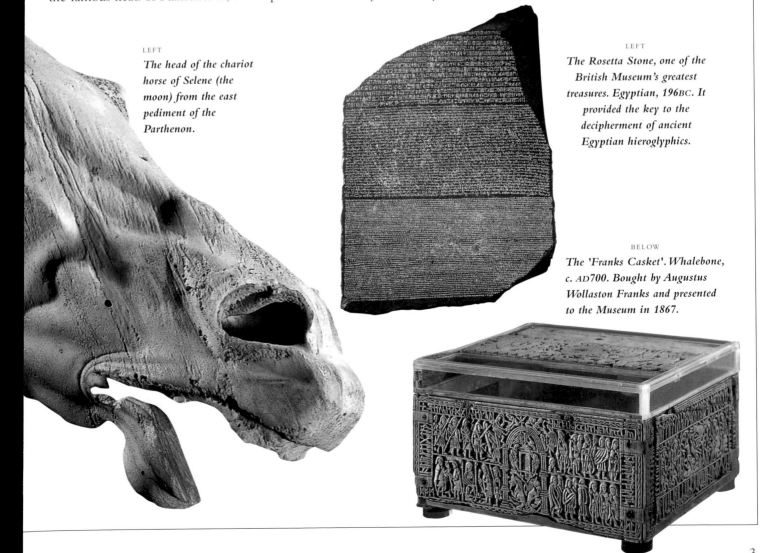

LEFT
*The head of the chariot horse of Selene (the moon) from the east pediment of the Parthenon.*

LEFT
*The Rosetta Stone, one of the British Museum's greatest treasures. Egyptian, 196BC. It provided the key to the decipherment of ancient Egyptian hieroglyphics.*

BELOW
*The 'Franks Casket'. Whalebone, c. AD700. Bought by Augustus Wollaston Franks and presented to the Museum in 1867.*

decided to erect a new building somewhat to the north of Montagu House and Sir Robert Smirke was chosen to design it. The form of the new museum was to consist of side- and top-lit galleries around a large courtyard. This was achieved by the early 1840s, and the last main part of the building to be constructed was the great portico with its fluted columns and ionic capitals. As the entrance front grew, so Montagu House was demolished. By 1850 the British Museum looked substantially as it does today.

The problems of space were not over, however. The famous Round Reading Room was built in the courtyard garden very shortly afterwards and it was open for readers by 1857. The natural history collections were also posing problems, and ultimately it was decided that they should be separated from the artefacts; they moved to South Kensington, in west London, in 1880. Although Smirke's new museum was still not big enough, a parliamentary commission of 1850 pointed out that some aspects of collecting were being insufficiently attended to. This led to the appointment of Augustus Wollaston Franks, a curator with a considerable breadth of interest and knowledge, who over nearly fifty years built up the collections of post-classical European antiquities, ethnography and oriental art. By the turn of the twentieth century, the British Museum had established the coverage of its collections in the way to which its founders had aspired, though in 1973 the decision was taken to divide the collections again, taking the books and manuscripts to form the new British Library.

What characterises the British Museum at the turn of the millennium? Most significant is the greater emphasis than hitherto on interpretation. Scholarship in historical and archaeological research, as well as scientific investigation, enables the Museum to adopt a multi-disciplinary approach well suited to its wide-ranging collections. Perhaps of even greater significance is the importance given by the Museum to the dissemination of that scholarship at many levels and to the widest possible audience, not only within the galleries of the Museum but far beyond them.

All this is not to say that collecting has been ignored. The late twentieth century has been a very active period, in particular with the acquisition of material culture by the Ethnography Department. The Museum has always relied heavily on private donations and bequests for acquisitions, and now has the additional support of bodies such as the

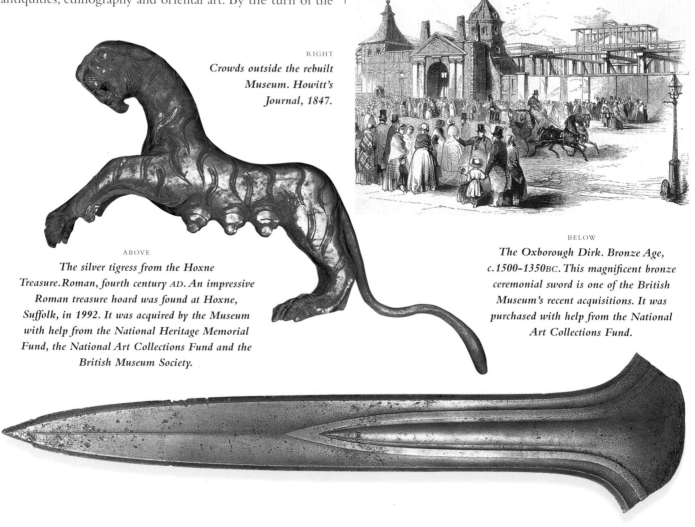

RIGHT
*Crowds outside the rebuilt Museum. Howitt's Journal, 1847.*

ABOVE
*The silver tigress from the Hoxne Treasure. Roman, fourth century AD. An impressive Roman treasure hoard was found at Hoxne, Suffolk, in 1992. It was acquired by the Museum with help from the National Heritage Memorial Fund, the National Art Collections Fund and the British Museum Society.*

BELOW
*The Oxborough Dirk. Bronze Age, c.1500–1350BC. This magnificent bronze ceremonial sword is one of the British Museum's recent acquisitions. It was purchased with help from the National Art Collections Fund.*

Heritage Lottery Fund, the National Heritage Memorial Fund, the National Art Collections Fund and the British Museum Society.

At the end of the century fieldwork and excavation are being pursued more actively than at any other time in the past. The aim of fieldwork is to conduct research and to add material to the collections that is representative of contemporary cultural practices, allowing the Museum to retain its claim to be a museum of world cultures past and present. This is largely, but not exclusively, pursued by the Ethnography Department, which has been active in parts of the world as diverse as Romania and New Guinea. Excavations are carried out by the Museum to increase knowledge and provide an invaluable method of adding new material to the collections, although not all finds come to the Museum. Traditionally excavations have been carried out by the British Museum in the Nile Valley (Egypt and the Sudan) and the Near East and this important work continues, often in collaboration with other bodies, but the British Museum also excavates sites in Britain as well as in other parts of the world. Evaluation of the discoveries made forms an important part of the work at the British Museum; the size and significance of a site can mean it will take many years to excavate and analyse fully.

ABOVE
*'Doctor' characters from the masquerade 'team' of Beresti village performing as part of a folk festival in Bacau, Moldavia, Romania in 1994. One of the masks from this group was later purchased from its maker for the Museum.*

The collections of the Museum are now divided between ten curatorial departments – Coins and Medals, Egyptian Antiquities, Ethnography, Greek and Roman Antiquities, Japanese Antiquities, Medieval and Later Antiquities, Oriental Antiquities, Prehistoric and Romano-British Antiquities, Prints and Drawings, and Western Asiatic Antiquities – each headed by a Keeper who has overall responsibility for the care, presentation and documentation of the objects. Taken together the collections of the British Museum make it perhaps the best single introduction to world cultures and civilisations that exists today.

## LEARNING AND TEACHING

Relatively few objects enter the collections of the British Museum with their identity certain and their history completely known. It is the task of the Museum to learn as much as possible about each object and its context. Research is mostly undertaken by curators, but vital research work is also carried out by scientists and conservators. In addition, the Museum has an important role as a centre of scholarship for scholars the world over, who come to consult the collections and to exchange information. The Museum is a place of learning in the broadest sense, and all staff have a responsibility to share and disseminate their knowledge to any interested person. The general public and teaching professionals have access to subject experts through correspondence and departmental Student Rooms, and to up-to-date information through lectures, seminars, special exhibitions and extensive publication and education programmes.

ABOVE
*Scholars at work in the Horological Student Room.*

# THE ANCIENT NEAR EAST

IT WAS IN THE ancient Near East - the region stretching from the Persian Gulf in the east to Palestine and Anatolia in the West – that the first signs of the 'Neolithic revolution' appeared: the beginnings of agriculture, the manufacture of pottery and the first steps towards urbanisation were accompanied by trade in rare goods such as obsidian, bitumen and lapis lazuli. This in turn led to the development of craft skills, and by 3500BC mining, smelting and the working of metals had been mastered.

The first true city-dwellers lived in Mesopotamia, the region between the Tigris and Euphrates rivers, during the fourth millennium BC. Centred around their temples, Sumerian cities of the third millennium BC

appear to have been theocratic states governed by rulers who were more priests than kings.

Excavations at the wealthy Sumerian city of Ur in the 1920s revealed a series of magnificent burials suggesting the existence of a powerful ruling class. Vast pits containing objects of tremendous wealth and beauty also held the bodies of the main occupants and up to seventy-four attendants – soldiers, musicians and maid-servants – as well as ox-drawn chariots.

Control of Mesopotamia was an elusive prize vied for by many cities: the Akkadians, Assyrians and Babylonians were all successful contestants in the years up to 1500BC. However, powerful civilisations were developing in other parts of the region. In Anatolia the Hittites established an empire that

NEOLITHIC

POTTERY NEOLITHIC

PRE-POTTERY NEOLITHIC

7000BC                6000BC                5000BC

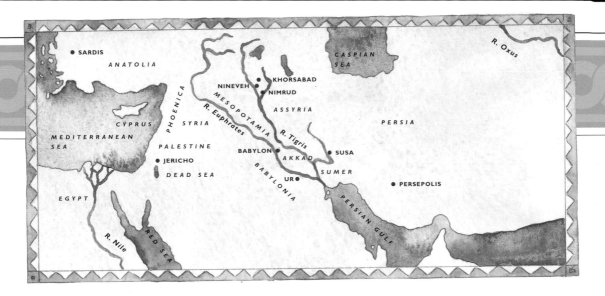

stretched into Syria as far as the borders of Egyptian-controlled Palestine, whose city-states – well positioned for trade with both Egypt and Mesopotamia – also enjoyed some military and economic weight in the area. In the early first millennium, the Assyrians rose to prominence once more: ruling from their magnificent capitals at Nimrud, Khorsabad and Nineveh, they dominated the Near East for three cen-turies before a resurgent Babylonia under King Nabopolassar defeated them and took over their empire.

Mesopotamian societies were the first to be literate. Writing started in Sumer, with the development of straightforward symbols used for accounting purposes: an ox's head to indicate an ox, a rising sun for a day, and so forth, and circles and half-circles for numbers.

By the early third millennium, these symbols, impressed on wet clay with the wedge-shaped end of a reed stylus, had become highly stylised and unrecognisable as pictures. Syllabic symbols developed from these 'cuneiform' patterns made it possible to write in sentences and express ideas. ▶

LEFT
*The Flood Tablet. From the library of Ashurbanipal at Nineveh, 7th century BC. Inscribed in cuneiform with the Babylonian version of the Biblical story of the Flood, this tablet highlights the common ground between Semitic religions and mythologies.*

ABOVE
*Plastered skull with shell-inlaid eyes. From Jericho, 7th millennium BC. This may have been connected with some form of ancestor cult.*

BELOW
*Clay tablet. From Ur, c. 2900–2600BC. The inscription in cuneiform script records deliveries of barley and meal to a temple.*

| | CHALCOLITHIC | EARLY BRONZE AGE | MIDDLE BRONZE AGE | LATE BRONZE AGE & AMARNAG PERIOD | ASSYRIAN ▶ |
| --- | --- | --- | --- | --- | --- |
| | | | | | IRON AGE |

3000BC        2000BC        1000BC

# THE ANCIENT NEAR EAST

Although it is quite a complex system, cuneiform became the all-purpose script of the Near East, adapted to the writing of many different languages. A vast range of written material survives on clay and stone, including diplomatic letters, astrological and mathematical texts, annals and mythological tales, laws and decrees.

The mid-first millennium BC saw the eclipse of the old powers of the Near East at the hands of Persia, though it was their neighbours

the Medes who first extended their dominion beyond present-day Iran into eastern Anatolia. In the sixth century the Persian king Cyrus defeated the Medes and took over their territories. Building himself a grand capital at Pasargadae, he subsequently captured Babylon and established an empire stretching from the Mediterranean to eastern Iran. Later Darius was to cement this huge inheritance by crushing rebellion and establishing a system of 'satraps', or local governors. His lavish building

ABOVE
*Ivory carving. From Nimrud, 800-750BC.*
*This Phoenician-style ivory, once*
*decorated with gold leaf and inlays of lapis*
*lazuli and carnelian, shows a Nubian boy*
*being attacked by a lioness.*

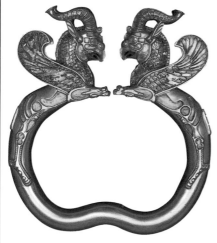

ABOVE AND RIGHT
*The Oxus Treasure.*
*Achaemenid-Persian, c. 550-400BC.*
*Gold bracelet with two leaping*
*griffins and gold model of a*
*four-horse chariot, part of a*
*collection of precious objects allegedly*
*discovered on the banks of the*
*River Oxus in 1880.*

| ASSYRIAN AND BABYLONIAN EMPIRES | | | | SELEUCID ERA | | |
|---|---|---|---|---|---|---|
| | | ACHAEMENID EMPIRE | | | PARTHIAN ERA | |
| 700BC | 600BC | 500BC | 400BC | 300BC | 200BC | 100BC |

projects included a new capital at Persepolis and the 'Royal Road' between Susa and Sardis.

Although Persian power was at its height, neither Darius nor his successor Xerxes was able to conquer mainland Greece, despite sustained attempts in the early fifth century BC. (The splendour and wealth of their rule made the name of the kings of Persia – more frequently simply 'the King' – a byword for luxury and power among Greeks.) Meanwhile, Persian subjugation of the Greek cities of the Aegean coast of Anatolia continued to rankle. In 334BC Alexander the Great crossed into Asia, liberated the Greek cities and plunged into the heart of the Persian empire, finally defeating and killing its ruler Darius III

*ABOVE*
***Bronze figure of a winged bull with human torso. From Urartu, c. 700BC.***

in 331. Crowned King of Persia, he married a Persian princess and proclaimed the unity of the Greeks and Persians – though he did not scruple to burn Persepolis.

After Alexander's death his empire crumbled; much of the Near Eastern parts came into the hands of the Seleucid dynasty, who founded Greek cities, spreading Greek culture as far east as the Hindu Kush and even into India. However, most of the population was unaffected, and when the Seleucids lost Persia to a Parthian dynasty from the north in 238BC, the area remained as hostile to Western powers as ever. Rome was destined to fight several bitter wars against the Parthians and their successors, the Sasanians, who retained control of the region until the Islamic conquest of AD651.

## ASSYRIAN PALACE RELIEFS

The Neo-Assyrian kings, who controlled the Near East from Egypt to the Persian Gulf from the ninth to the seventh century BC, ruled from a series of capitals at Nimrud, Khorsabad and Nineveh. The centrepieces of these cities were the great royal palaces, with their monumental gateways protected by winged, human-headed bulls and their walls lined with carved stone slabs showing royal exploits such as hunting and warfare. The British Museum is the only place where so many sequences of these magnificently preserved slabs can be seen in their original order. Excavated between 1845 and 1855, mostly by Sir Henry Layard, they include the famous reliefs of King Ashurbanipal hunting lions from his palace at Nineveh (c. 645BC).

| ROMAN EMPIRE | | | BYZANTINE EMPIRE | | | |
|---|---|---|---|---|---|---|
| | | SASANIAN EMPIRE | | | | ARAB CONQUEST & ISLAMIC ERA |
| AD100 | AD200 | AD300 | AD400 | AD500 | AD600 | AD700 |

THE HISTORY of Islam began in Arabia in AD622, when the Prophet Muhammad migrated from Mecca to Medina and established a community of believers there. Following the death of the Prophet in 632, the leadership of the Islamic community passed to a series of Caliphs, the second of whom, Umar, undertook the active conversion of neighbouring lands to Islam. After the death of Umar, the Caliphate passed first to Uthman, then to Ali, the Prophet's nephew, and from him to another branch of the family, the Umayyads. The Umayyads ruled from Damascus until the mid-eighth century, when they were defeated by the Abbasids of Baghdad. By this time, the weakened Byzantine, Visigothic and Sasanian empires had succumbed to the Muslim armies, and the Islamic world stretched from Afghanistan, Iran and Iraq in the east via Syria, Egypt and the North African coast as far as Spain in the west. Great cities

ABOVE

*Gold dinar of the Abbasid Caliph al-Musta'sim, AD1242–58. There are many different ways of ornamenting Kufic script. The end of the letters on this coin are extended as foliage.*

arose, and mosques and universities were built as centres for Islamic learning.

Many of the regions converted to Islam had venerable traditions of their own: since the mid-first millennium BC, southern Arabia had itself been the home of ancient Semitic kingdoms such as Saba, Qataban and Hadhramaut. Far from ignoring these pre-Islamic cultures, the Arab conquerors used them to their advantage: in Syria and Iran, for example, the new Islamic regimes were openly built on the foundations of the Greco-Roman and Sasanian cultures. This openness also extended to learning: Greek scientific and mathematical manuscripts were preserved, translated and copied by Arab and Iranian scholars, while being ignored in Medieval Europe.

Nonetheless, the art of the Islamic world soon developed

ABOVE

*Brass ewer inlaid with silver. From Herat, Afghanistan, c. AD1200. The high degree of skill achieved by Islamic metalworkers can be seen in the inlaid decoration and the relief figures of birds and lions.*

## THE ISLAMIC FAITH

Muslims believe that the faith of Islam – which means 'submission' – was divinely revealed to the Prophet Muhammad, who had it set down in the holy book, known as the Quran. They believe in one God and acknowledge the Old Testament prophets and Jesus, though as another prophet, not the Son of God. There is no priesthood in Islam, although there are religious scholars who give legal and theological opinions, and most mosques have an imam to lead prayers. All Muslims must observe the 'Five Pillars' of Islam. The first of these is the affirmation that there is only one God and that the Prophet Muhammad is the Messenger of God. The second is prayer. The third is almsgiving, the fourth fasting during the holy month of Ramadan and the fifth to make, if possible, the Pilgrimage to Mecca.

ABOVE

*Brass astrolabe. From Iran, AD1712. The astrolabe was especially important in Muslim society as it was used to give the times and direction of prayer (performed five times a day while facing Mecca). This magnificent example was made for the Safavid ruler Shah Sultan Husayn.*

| MIGRATION OF THE PROPHET MUHAMMAD TO MEDINA AD622 | DEATH OF MUHAMMAD AD632 | ABBASIDS AD749–1258 BAGHDAD |
| THE 'ORTHODOX CALIPHS' AD632–661 | UMAYYADS AD661–750 | FATIMIDS AD969–1171 CAIRO |

| AD600 | AD700 | AD800 | AD900 | AD1000 | AD1100 | AD1200 |

10

some common characteristics. In a world bound together by the written word, calligraphy assumed the highest importance, and even the briefest texts, such as imperial monograms, were executed with the greatest attention to design. Typical of the early Islamic period, the elegant, angular Kufic script was somewhat eclipsed in later times by the flowing Naskhi and Thuluth styles. Another characteristic was the avoidance of human and animal figures in religious contexts, which encouraged the use of geometric and abstract design, including the graceful stylised plant motifs known as arabesques.

The non-representational nature of much Islamic art led to an emphasis on the decorative arts – in textile, ceramic, glass, metal and other media. From the ninth century, trade with the East introduced Chinese silks and porcelains, which were to have a profound effect on textile and ceramic design. Trade with Europe also led to the cross-fertilisation of ideas; for example, Islamic exports inspired the Venetian enamelled-glass industry and encouraged the use of precious-metal inlays in brass vessels.

The second half of the millennium saw the establishment of larger empires and more enduring dynasties. Among them were the Ottomans, conquerors of the eastern Byzantine territories and the Mamluk empire, who made Istanbul their capital in 1453; the Safavids, who ruled Iran from the sixteenth to the eighteenth century; their successors, the Qajars, who lasted into the twentieth century; and the Mughals who controlled much of India between the sixteenth and nineteenth century.

ABOVE

*Carved marble panel from a cenotaph. From Cairo, AD967. Strict Islamic observance forbids the construction of elaborate tombs, so the deceased were often commemorated with cenotaphs instead. The majestic Kufic inscription reads 'In the Name of God the Merciful'.*

ABOVE

*Glass mosque lamp. From Egypt or Syria, AD1330–35. The Mamluk Sultans ruled Egypt and Syria from the mid-13th to the early 16th century, and large numbers of enamelled and gilded glass lamps were commissioned for the many mosques they and their court officials built in Cairo.*

LEFT

*Ceramic basin. From Iznik, Turkey, AD1530–40. Made in the famous Iznik potteries, this large footed basin is elaborately decorated with swirling blossoms and leaves painted in underglaze purple, green, blue and black.*

MAMLUKS AD1250–1517 CAIRO

❖ OTTOMANS CONQUER ISTANBUL AD1453

SAFAVIDS AD1501–1722/65

MUGHALS AD1526–1858 DELHI, AGRA

OTTOMANS C. AD1281–1924

QAJARS AD1779–1925

| AD1400 | AD1500 | AD1600 | AD1700 | AD1800 | AD1900 |

# AFRICA

ALTHOUGH THE question of where the earliest humans lived may never be entirely settled, Africa certainly provides us with some of the earliest evidence of their activities. Stoneworking began just over two million years ago, and long stretches of its development can be observed at Olduvai Gorge in Tanzania, where among the earliest stone tools produced were large hand axes. Although these could be quite versatile, a major breakthrough came around 120,000 years ago with a technological development that enabled the manufacture of smaller, more precise flint blades – ranging from sizeable spear-heads to tiny 'microliths' – which could be fitted to shafts of wood,

*ABOVE*
**'Tulip' beaker. From Kush,
c. 1750–1550BC. This hand-formed
beaker was found in a tomb alongside
other artefacts intended to assist the
deceased in the afterlife.**

bone or antler to create useful tools for hunting and gathering food. Around the same time, the first art appeared in the shape of cave paintings and small carvings.

Conditions in the fertile Nile Valley, close to the technologically advanced Near East, led to the rapid domestication of animals and the development of agriculture. Around 3100BC the lower Nile Valley and Delta were consolidated to form the land of Egypt, which remained the dominant influence in the region for several millennia.

Artistic expression reached great levels of sophistication, with the construction of very elaborate tombs and temples and the production of fine sculptures, wall paintings, ceramics and jewellery.

A GROUP – A HORIZON
3500–2800BC

5000BC     4500BC     4000BC     3500BC     3000BC     2500BC

The relationship between Egypt and its southern neighbours was volatile. Nubia, and more particularly the kingdom of Kush, whose capital was at Kerma, played a vital role in supplying Egypt with gold and African luxury goods such as ivory, ebony, incense and exotic animal skins. However, although Egypt intermittently controlled the region, Kush was itself a strong and organised society, and in the eighth century BC the tables were turned when a powerful Kushite dynasty from Napata succeeded in conquering Egypt, establishing the twenty-fifth dynasty.

Although its rule in Egypt lasted less than a century, Kush – renamed Meroë after its new capital – remained a major power for another thousand years. Like its predecessors, Meroë thrived on trade and war, causing grave problems for the Romans who colonised much of North Africa between the second and first centuries BC. The art of Meroë was heavily influenced by that of Egypt and Rome, and Meroitic royalty were buried in pyramid tombs. In the third century AD, however, Meroë was eclipsed by the Christian state of Aksum in northern Ethiopia, which became the main route for trade between central Africa and the Mediterranean.

The later part of the first millennium AD saw the loosening of links between northern and sub-Saharan Africa; as the desert expanded, contact was increasingly restricted to ▶

LEFT
*Sandstone carving. From Faras, 7th century AD. Part of a frieze from the first Christian cathedral at Faras, showing the Christian cross above a bird's head.*

BELOW
*Pottery bowls. From Faras, 'C Group'. Pottery was produced in the Nile Valley from Neolithic times onward. These polished and incised wares typify the local style of Lower Nubia.*

ABOVE
*Wall painting. From Thebes, Egypt, New Kingdom, c. 1400BC. This wall painting from a tomb chapel shows Nubians presenting African products – including gold, incense and animal skins – to the Egyptian pharaoh.*

| C GROUP – C HORIZON 2300–1500BC | | NAPATAN PERIOD 1000–300BC | MEROITIC PERIOD 300BC–AD350 | | CHRISTIAN PERIOD AD550–1500 | |
| --- | --- | --- | --- | --- | --- | --- |
| | NEW KINGDOM – EGYPTIAN OCCUPATION 1550–1069BC | | | | | |
| KERMA 2500–1500BC | | 25TH DYNASTY NUBIAN RULE OVER EGYPT 747–656BC | | X GROUP – X GROUP, NOBA, BALLANA AD350–550 | | ISLAMIC PERIOD AD1500– |

| 1500BC | 1000BC | 500BC | 0 | AD500 | AD1000 | AD1500 |

coastal regions. North Africa embraced first Christianity, then Islam, leading to the establishment of great Arab cities such as Cairo in Egypt, Fes in Morocco and Kairouan in Tunisia. By the eighteenth century Islam had spread into West Africa, becoming the main religion among the great empires of Tekrur, Ghana, Songhay and Mali, where Timbuktu became a noted centre of Islamic scholarship. By the beginning of the second millennium AD prosperous Muslim communities were already becoming established along the East African coast. In all these areas Islamic strictures against representational art led to a focus on architectural decoration, leatherwork and textiles.

In the non-Muslim kingdoms of West Africa, certain valuable objects and materials – especially metals – were the prerogative of kings and chiefs. Indeed, the institution of kingship, which dates from the early second millennium AD, was closely connected with the production and control of metals. In Ghana, for example, the kings and chiefs of the Asante people once controlled the local gold trade as a means of obtaining firearms from European traders. They still make extensive use of local gold in their elaborate regalia, while miniature brass sculptures of humans and animals are used as weights for measuring gold dust. In Nigeria, craftsmen attached to the courts of Benin and Ife produced finely detailed cast bronzes and ivory carvings. In some cases, the supernatural powers of a ruler were considered to render him potentially dangerous to his subjects; thus royal and divine imagery is often closely connected.

Such religious thinking played an important role in African material culture generally, and especially in the art of the peoples inhabiting the dense forest regions stretching along the southern coast of West Africa to the Congo basin. The relative isolation of these communities

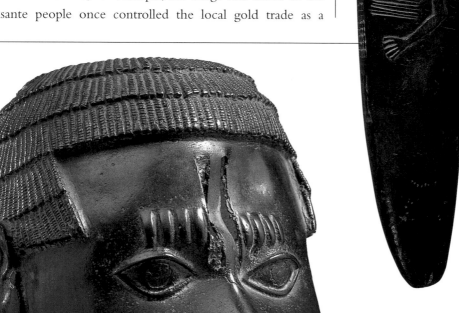

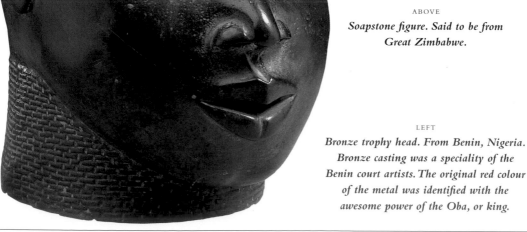

ABOVE
*Soapstone figure. Said to be from Great Zimbabwe.*

LEFT
*Bronze trophy head. From Benin, Nigeria. Bronze casting was a speciality of the Benin court artists. The original red colour of the metal was identified with the awesome power of the Oba, or king.*

resulted in a wide variety of local styles. Prolific wood carvers, they mainly produced religious images and masks, which play an important ritual role in many parts of Africa and are regarded as objects of great power.

In the forests and savannahs of central Africa, wood carvers tended to produce more decorative items such as cups, furniture and boxes, although the Kuba of the Democratic Republic of Congo are also noted for their masks and the fine sculpted figures of their kings. Elsewhere in eastern and southern Africa, there is a more apparent emphasis on bodily decoration, though the warriors of the Masai, Zulu and Matabele peoples also take pride in their elaborate shields and weapons. Parts of South Africa and the Sahara are famous for their sites containing painted rock surfaces; some of these are certainly of antiquity, but by no means all.

The first direct documented contacts between European traders and sub-Saharan Africa came in the fifteenth century. In later centuries, European colonisation and the forced deportation of thousands of Africans as slaves was to have a profound effect on the subsequent development of the American, Caribbean and British cultures. Just as in the 1920s African art provided inspiration to European painters and sculptors, so contemporary African artists are adopting and adapting European art forms to develop new expressions of their traditions.

LEFT
*Woven textile. From Tillaberi, Nigeria. Wool and goat hair, 20th century. African weavers used a variety of materials in their work, incorporating a wide vocabulary of patterns and motifs.*

ABOVE
*Wood mask. From Dan, Ivory Coast.*

LEFT
*Wood mask. From Guro, Ivory Coast. It appears to be in a form which mixes animal and human attributes and is associated with spirits of the bush.*

15

# EGYPT

In the sixth millennium BC, the people of the Nile valley began to take a different cultural path from the rest of Africa. Already skilled hunters and stone-workers, they began to turn their attention to the cultivation of the rich Nile silt. The establishment of settled communities led to the development of simple industries such as pottery-making and copper-smelting. By about 3600BC, these Predynastic Egyptians were hunting with sophisticated flint weapons, producing painted pottery and building shrines to the local deities who later made up the complex Egyptian pantheon. The earliest Egyptian writing appeared, rapidly developing into the largely phonetic hieroglyphic script used throughout later Egyptian history. The names of individual kings began to be recorded, including those of Narmer and Aha. Egyptian tradition records that a southern ruler gained control of the whole country around 3100BC and established the first national capital at Memphis, close to the junction of the Nile Valley and the Delta.

This symbolic unification of the 'Two Lands' of Upper Egypt - the Valley - and Lower Egypt - the Delta - was central to Egyptian ideas of kingship. Known as 'Pharaoh', meaning 'Great House', the king was regarded as both human and divine. In life, he was seen as the son of the sun-god Ra and the human incarnation of the falcon-god Horus; in death, as Osiris, the Lord of the Underworld. Temples to the gods were exploited as vehicles for royal propaganda, incorporating huge statues and relief carvings of the king in traditional attitudes as the unifier and defender of Egypt.

Long king-lists carved on the temple walls were tailored to political expediency; discredited kings – and all female rulers –

*RIGHT*
**Upper part of a colossal statue of the nineteenth-dynasty pharaoh Ramesses II, from his memorial temple at Thebes. New Kingdom, c. 1270BC. The inspiration for Shelley's poem 'Ozymandias', it was brought to the British Museum in 1818.**

*ABOVE*
**Ivory label showing the first-dynasty king Den striking an enemy. From his tomb at Abydos, Early Dynastic, c. 3000BC. Rulers of Egypt continued to be portrayed in this traditional attitude as the country's defender as late as Roman times.**

| PREDYNASTIC 5500–3100BC | | OLD KINGDOM 2686–2181BC | | MIDDLE KINGDOM 2055–1650BC |
| --- | --- | --- | --- | --- |
| | EARLY DYNASTIC 3100–2686BC | | 1ST INTERMEDIATE 2181–2055BC | 2ND INTERMEDIATE 1650–1550B |

3000BC      2500BC      2000BC

were simply removed from the official record. No attempt at writing history in the modern sense is known to have been made until around 250BC, when a priest called Manetho compiled a list of thirty Dynasties, or ruling families. Later historians grouped these into 'Kingdoms' – periods of relative stability – separated by 'Intermediate Periods' characterised by war or political fragmentation.

Despite the impression of continuity given by the use of traditional imagery in royal art, cultural and political alignments often changed, as indicated by the frequent shifts of adminstrative centre as dynasties from different localities came to power. These often reflected the ancient rivalry between the north and south: Thebes in Upper Egypt enjoyed prominence for extended periods during the Middle and New Kingdoms, but was eventually superseded by a series of Delta cities including Tanis.

Conquest by Persia in 525BC brought native Egyptian rule to an end, and in 332 Alexander the Great claimed Egypt as part of his empire. Following Alexander's death, ▶

LEFT

*Part of a king-list from the temple of Ramesses II at Abydos. New Kingdom, c. 1250BC. The hieroglyphs in the oval enclosures, or 'cartouches', spell out his name and those of previous pharaohs.*

RIGHT

*The Hunters' Palette. Predynastic, c. 3100BC. Egyptians protected their eyes by outlining them with black eyepaint called kohl. Inspired by the shape of the palettes used to prepare these cosmetics, the Hunters' Palette is carved with scenes of hunters and their prey, including lions and ostriches.*

ABOVE

*The Pitt-Rivers Knife. Predynastic, c. 3600–3250BC. he finely-worked flint blade fitted with an ivory handle rved with figures of animals.*

| NEW KINGDOM 1550–1069BC | | LATE PERIOD 747–332BC | | ROMAN 30BC–AD395 |
|---|---|---|---|---|
| | 3RD INTERMEDIATE 1069–747BC | | PTOLEMAIC 332–30BC | |

1000BC     500BC     0

# EGYPT

his general Ptolemy established his own dynasty. With a new capital at Alexandria on the northern coast, Egypt became increasingly involved in the cultural and political world of the Greek Mediterranean; this process intensified after 30BC, when the last Ptolemaic ruler, Cleopatra VII, was defeated by Octavian and Egypt became a part of the Roman Empire.

Although the Persian, Greek and Roman rulers had themselves represented in conventional pharaonic attitudes and found it expedient to support and build temples, they were less concerned with Egypt's religion and culture than its legendary wealth. At the height of its power during the New Kingdom, Egypt's empire had extended south to the fourth Nile cataract in Nubia and as far north as the modern-day border between Syria and

ABOVE

*Glazed composition hippopotamus decorated with aquatic plants. Middle Kingdom, c. 1900BC.*

Turkey. As well as controlling the trade in exotic goods from Africa – ebony, ivory and gold – Egypt produced such desirable export goods as linen, papyrus and grain – grain that Rome in particular needed to feed its expanding empire.

Much of what we know about the ancient Egyptians derives from their tombs and the artefacts placed in them for their owners to enjoy in the afterlife.

During the Early Dynastic period and Old Kingdom, mastaba tombs modelled on the homes of the living were constructed at such sites as Abydos in the south and Saqqara in the north. In the Old Kingdom, pharaohs were buried in enormous stone pyramid complexes like those at Giza, but from the New Kingdom onward, they preferred the greater security of tombs cut into the ground or hillside, as in the Valley of the Kings at Thebes.

## MUMMIFICATION

Egyptian cemeteries were commonly sited in the desert to the west of towns and cities. The earliest burials were made directly into pits in the ground, where they were preserved by the hot dry sand. A belief in life after death was current by Predynastic times when burials typically included simple grave goods.

To preserve the body as a home for the ka – the deceased's life force – the practice of mummification was developed. After the removal of the internal organs – which were separately preserved in four containers known as Canopic jars – the body was dried out using natron, a natural salt. Finally it was

wrapped in linen bandages and placed in a coffin. As incarnate gods, the pharaohs underwent especially elaborate mummification. They were carefully bandaged with fine linen, their bodies covered with

protective amulets and jewellery. A gold mask was placed over the neck and head before the royal mummy was encased in a series of coffins and placed in a huge stone sarcophagus in the burial chamber.

BELOW

*Mummy of the twenty-second dynasty Theban priestess Tjentmutengebtiu. Late Period, c. 900BC. The coffin is painted with protective images and figures of deities.*

Paintings and reliefs inside the royal tombs illustrate the complex funerary beliefs of the ancient Egyptians; however, it was only with the decipherment of the accompanying texts in the nineteenth century that these began to be understood. Royal tomb paintings often depict the strange geography and terrifying creatures of the underworld, which the sungod travelled through at night. After death the soul followed the sun through the underworld and entered the court of the god Osiris. Here the deceased's heart was weighed to ascertain its righteousness; if it passed the test, the soul would achieve a peaceful afterlife in the god's estates. ▶

ABOVE

*Glazed composition amulet comprising the hieroglyphs for 'life, stability and power'. Late Period, c. 700-500BC.*

RIGHT

*Head of a colossal red granite statue of Amenophis III. From Karnak, eighteenth dynasty, c.1390BC. The crowned head is nearly 3 metres high.*

## DYNASTIES

**First Dynasty** c. 3100–2890BC

**Second Dynasty** c. 2890–2686BC

**Third Dynasty** c. 2686–2613BC

**Fourth Dynasty** c. 2613–2494BC

**Fifth Dynasty** c. 2494–2345BC

**Sixth Dynasty** c. 2345–2181BC

**Seventh/Eighth Dynasty**
c. 2181–2125BC

**Ninth/Tenth Dynasty**
c. 2160–2130BC, c. 2125–2025BC

**Eleventh Dynasty** c. 2125–1985BC

**Twelfth Dynasty** c. 1985–1795BC

**Thirteenth Dynasty**
c. 1795–1650BC

**Fourteenth Dynasty**
c. 1750–1650BC

**Fifteenth Dynasty
(Hyksos)**
c. 1650–1550BC

**Sixteenth Dynasty**
c. 1650–c. 1550BC

**Seventeenth Dynasty**
c. 1650–1550BC

**Eighteenth Dynasty**
c. 1550–1295BC

**Nineteenth Dynasty**
c. 1295–1186BC

**Twentieth Dynasty**
c. 1186–1069BC

**Twenty-first Dynasty**
c. 1069–945BC

**Twenty-second Dynasty**
c. 945–715BC

**Twenty-third Dynasty** c. 818–715BC

**Twenty-fourth Dynasty**
c. 727–715BC

**Twenty-fifth Dynasty
(Nubian or Kushite)**
c. 747–656BC

**Twenty-sixth Dynasty
(Saite)**
c. 664–525BC

**Twenty-seventh Dynasty
(Persian Kings)**
c. 525–404BC

**Twenty-eighth Dynasty** c. 404–399BC

**Twenty-ninth Dynasty** c. 399–380BC

**Thirtieth Dynasty** c. 380–343BC

**Persian Kings** c. 343–332BC

**Macedonian Kings** c. 332–305BC

**The Ptolemies** c. 305–30BC

**Roman Emperors** 30BC–AD395

# EGYPT

In many periods the tombs of commoners were carved and painted with vivid scenes of everyday life. These were not meant just for decoration; like all Egyptian funerary art, their purpose was in part to provide the deceased magically with everything required for the afterlife. New Kingdom paintings of officials supervising agricultural activities or enjoying family parties, for example, were created to allow them to enjoy their earthly status and pleasures in the next world. In addition, tombs were stocked with all the necessities of life – food, clothing, cosmetics, jewellery, writing materials and furniture; often preserved intact by Egypt's dry climate, these provide valuable information about the details of ancient Egyptian life. Specifically funerary objects included models of boats, animals and servants, and amulets to protect the body. Papyrus scrolls, or 'Books of the Dead', were books of spells to help the dead in the afterlife.

Very little material survives outside tombs and temples, but some sites have provided objects straight from daily life, and a mass of texts ranging from laundry lists to letters and literary compositions.

LEFT

*Gilded inner coffin of Henutmehyt, a priestess of the god Amun during the reign of Ramesses II. Nineteenth dynasty, c. 1290BC.*

RIGHT

*Wall painting from the tomb of Nebamun, an eighteenth-dynasty Theban official. New Kingdom, c. 1390BC. The scene represents a banquet, with musicians and dancers.*

RIGHT

*Papyrus Book of the Dead written for the nineteenth-dynasty royal scribe Any. New Kingdom, c. 1250BC. 'Books of the Dead', known to the Egyptians as the 'Chapters of Coming Forth by Day' were collections of magic spells and instructions intended to guide and protect the deceased in the afterlife.*

LEFT

*Painted wooden box containing shabtis made for the nineteenth-dynasty Theban priestess Henutmehyt. Shabtis were magical figurines placed in the tomb to work on behalf of the deceased in the next world.*

# EGYPTIAN RELIGION

The Egyptian religion was a system of ancient cults based around the natural cycles on which Egypt's agricultural economy depended. Deities personifying these natural forces were often worshipped in local 'triads' comprising a god, his spouse and their child, for example Ptah, Sekhmet and Nefertum at Memphis, Osiris, Isis and Horus at Abydos and Amun, Mut and Khons at Thebes. Many deities took the form of birds or animals, for example the falcon Horus or the lioness Sekhmet. Some were bird- or animal-headed humans. Others, such as Ptah and Osiris, were always shown as humans. As the intermediary between the gods and humanity, the pharaoh was responsible for maintaining earthly and divine order, personified by the goddess Maat; to please the other deities and enlist their support in this task, vast temples dedicated to them were built throughout Egypt.

*Evidence of the Late Period animal cults. The bronze Gayer Anderson Cat, after 600BC, represents the goddess Bastet; a silvered pectoral bears the sacred eye of Horus. The intricately wrapped mummy of a cat is from Abydos. Roman Period, after 30BC.*

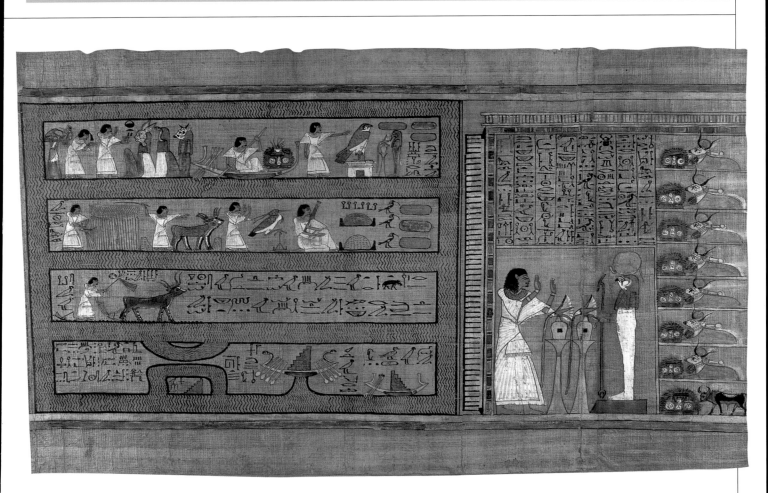

# CHINA

ICE WAS CULTIVATED along China's fertile south-east coast by 5000BC. Settled societies grew up, developing distinctive traits expressed in jade carving and the production of ritual and decorative ceramics.

Later tradition dated the earliest ruling dynasty, the Xia, to the period around 2000BC, but the first dynasty for which there is archaeological evidence is the Shang, who came to power about 1500BC. The large, well-defined Shang capitals in the Yellow River valley were equipped with palaces and temples and surrounded by rich burial sites. The use of bronze for weaponry, ornament and ritual was central to the Shang and their successors. During the Shang and Western Zhou periods, great numbers of bronze vessels and weapons were buried in tombs and hoards, while valuable bronze artefacts were dedicated to ancestors in the hope of their assistance or in gratitude for services performed.

The Shang period also saw the earliest use of writing in the form of inscribed oracle bones and shells. This written system was to prove one of the most important instruments in creating a unified Chinese cultural tradition; even today, many of the ancient characters remain in use. Under the Eastern Zhou (770-221BC), ink and bamboo were used to record rituals, political proceedings, history and philosophy, marking the beginning of the Chinese literary tradition.

LEFT

*Wooden guardian figure, crowned by antlers made of dry lacquer. Eastern Zhou period, 4th-3rd century BC. Wooden figures with monstrous faces, long tongues and antlers were placed as guardians in Chu tombs in southern Henan and northern Hubei provinces. This example is one of very few such artefacts surviving today.*

ABOVE

*Carvings in jade and other hard stones. Neolithic, c. 3500BC. Jades such as these are thought to have been made for ceremonial purposes and to have a protective function, warding off evil spirits both in life and after death.*

◀ NEOLITHIC (TO 1500BC) • SHANG (C.1500-1050BC)    WESTERN ZHOU (1050-771BC)

EASTERN ZHOU (770-221BC)
SPRING AND AUTUMN PERIOD(770-475BC)

| 1200BC | 1100BC | 1000BC | 900BC | 800BC | 700BC | 600BC |

In 221BC, following a period of violent civil discord and inter-state rivalry, Qin Shi Huangdi succeeded in uniting the whole of China, ushering in the imperial period. Although the dynasty he founded was short-lived, the Qin government left a lasting legacy in the form of a reformed writing system, a network of roads, a unified coinage and a standardised system of weights and measures. The Qin also made one of the first attempts to construct a 'Great Wall' in the north; intended to exclude the nomad tribes of the steppes beyond, this long border defence was created by linking short sections of wall built by previous regimes.

The Qin was overthrown by the Han dynasty (206BC-AD220) whose reign continued the development of the bureaucracy so characteristic of imperial China. Men were largely recruited on the basis of personal recommendation, but military skill and literary ability were the qualities which helped an individual's advance. In the early empire, guidance on the conduct of government was provided by two widely diverging philosophies, Confucianism and Daoism. Confucius (551-479BC) was a philosopher and teacher of political conduct whose doctrines emphasised moral order, the strict observance of ritual and tradition, and the cultivation of the civilised arts. Daoism, on the other hand, advocated the 'Way of Heaven', the path of harmony with nature and the cosmos. Best known through the works of Lao Zi (c. 604-531BC), the ultimate goal of Daoism is immortality, attained through control of the mind and attunement to the infinite.

Following the collapse of the Han dynasty, the north underwent a period of fragmentation and foreign rule. This political decentralisation coincided with the spread of Buddhism, brought to China by Indian monks via the Silk Route. This great trade route connected South Asia ▶

ABOVE
*Bronze ritual vessel. Early-middle Western Zhou period (1050-771BC). This inscribed vessel was cast for the Duke of Xing, a descendant of the famous historical figure, the Duke of Zhou. Large bronzes tended to be used for ritual and ceremonial purposes and have been excavated in vast quantities from various burial sites.*

BELOW
*Silver comb with repoussé decoration of birds and flowers, enhanced with gilding. Tang/Liao dynasty, c. AD618-1125. Hair ornaments and buckles were two of the main forms of personal adornment in China.*

QIN 221-207BC

SOUTHERN AND NORTHERN DYNASTIES (AD265-581)
THREE KINGDOMS (AD221-280)

WARRING STATES (475-221BC)

WESTERN HAN (206BC-AD9)     XIN (AD9-25)     EASTERN HAN (AD25-220)

400BC          300BC          200BC          100BC          BC/AD          AD100          AD200

# CHINA

and China with the Mediterranean world via the oases of Central Asia. Important centres of art and trade developed at Kashgar and Dunhuang, where the artistic influences of Gandhara and Kashmir can be seen in rock-cut monasteries and stupas, wall paintings and religious sculptures. This Central Asian art in turn exerted a profound influence on the Buddhist art of northern China between the fourth and sixth centuries AD.

In AD589 China was reunified under the Sui dynasty, whose rulers patronised Buddhism as a state religion. They in turn were followed by the Tang (AD618-906), whose magnificent court was famous as a centre of the arts. The importance of trade along the Silk Route is reflected in the glazed earthenware models of horses and camels, as well as silver vessels.

During the succeeding Song dynasty (960-1279), control of the north became difficult due to constant foreign incursions; eventually in 1127 a Jurchen invasion from the north-east forced the Song rulers to retreat southwards.

Henceforth the capital of north China was sited at Beijing, and it was here that the Mongols later established their capital Khambaliq to rule the whole of China. However, despite the northern threat, this southern Song period was one of intense intellectual and cultural activity, much of it directed towards understanding Chinese history and the role of the state. Confucian thought underwent a revival, and new editions of the Confucian canon were published, taking advantage of the newly developed technique of printing.

**RIGHT**
*Stoneware figure from a judgement group. Ming dynasty, 16th century AD. The belief in hell entered China with Buddhism during the early first millennium AD. From the late Tang dynasty such statues depicting characters from the underworld were common.*

SOUTHERN AND NORTHERN DYNASTIES (AD265-581)

TANG (AD618-906)

LIAO (AD907-1125)

SUI (AD589-618)

FIVE DYNASTIES (AD907-960)

NORTHERN SONG (AD960-1126)

SOUTHERN SONG (AD1127-1279)

AD500          AD600          AD700          AD800          AD900          AD1000          AD1100

A huge market existed for these printed editions of the scriptures, since they formed the syllabus of a state-run examination system which had started and developed during the Sui and Tang dynasties. The Song interest in past tradition had its counterpart in the decorative arts. The influence of early jades and bronzes, for example, can be seen in the heavy, rounded shape of Song stonewares, while the fine porcelains often mimic the elegant forms of beaten gold and silver vessels.

With the end of the Mongol rule in the fourteenth century, imperial power passed to another native dynasty, the Ming (AD1368–1644), who

established their capital at Nanjing for a brief period before moving it back to Beijing. Building on techniques developed by the Yuan, Ming artists produced porcelains painted with underglaze blue or overglaze enamel colours, spectacular carved lacquer wares, cloisonné enamels and gilt-bronze sculptures. However, in 1644 Manchurian invaders from the north ousted the Ming, establishing the last imperial dynasty, the Qing, who ruled until 1911.

As in earlier times, Qing art reflected a deep respect for the past, favouring traditional forms and techniques, though there were also numerous innovations, especially in the development of the decorative arts, notably the *famille verte* and *famille rose* enamel palette.

LEFT
*Porcelain dish painted with a fish among water plants. Yuan dynasty, 14th century AD. Overseas trade boomed during the Yuan dynasty. Among the imports from Iran was cobalt. Its use in the first quarter of the 14th century on the high-quality white porcelain from Jingdezhen had a fundamental impact on ceramics throughout the world.*

ABOVE
*Hell money, 20th century AD. It is traditional at Chinese New Year to burn imitation bank notes printed in the name of the Bank of Hell as offerings to the ancestors in the Spirit World.*

| | | | | | | PEOPLE'S REPUBLIC (AD1949-) |
| JIN (AD1115-1234) | | MING (AD1368-1644) | | | | |
| | YUAN (AD1279-1368) | | | | QING (AD1644-1911) | REPUBLIC (1912-1949) |
| AD1300 | AD1400 | AD1500 | AD1600 | AD1700 | AD1800 | AD1900 |

# SOUTH ASIA

Although evidence of artistic activity in India dates from the eighth millennium BC, the earliest complex urban civilisation flourished in the Indus Valley in the third millennium BC. The three main cities – Harappa, Mohenjo-Daro and Kalibangan – were large and well-planned, and excavations have yielded quantities of pottery, terracotta figures and stone and copper tools.

From around 2000BC city life began to decline and human activity retreated to rural villages; copper remained the principal functional material until iron replaced it around 1000BC. A second period of urbanisation began around 800BC: the resulting growth in the wealth and influence of specific centres led to the birth of dynastic states and small republics. The northern part of the subcontinent was populated by speakers of the Indo-European languages from which Sanskrit and modern north Indian tongues descend, and with these languages came an oral religious tradition. It was an age of philosophical and religious enquiry, from which emerged not only the complex and highly regulated Hindu religion, but also the alternative systems proposed by the Buddha and Mahavira, the founder of the Jain faith.

In the third century BC King Asoka Maurya united northern India, using Buddhism to expand his empire and to legitimise its power. The fall of the Mauryans initiated a period of fragmentation, although Buddhism retained a wide following. The Kushan era of the first to third century AD saw a flourishing of Buddhist art in Gandhara, while the contemporary Satavahana dynasty in the Deccan created the rich sculptures of

LEFT
*The Buddha. From Sarnath, Uttar Pradesh. Sandstone, 5th–6th century AD.*
*The Buddha was a religious teacher of the 6th century BC who gave up the privileges of noble birth to seek spiritual enlightenment, or nirvana.*

ABOVE RIGHT
*Tara. From Sri Lanka. Gilded bronze, 8th century AD. Tara is the greatest of all Buddhist goddesses and has a wide cult following. Here she makes the gesture of gift-giving or charity with her right hand.*

ABOVE
*Stamp seal. From the Indus Valley. Steatite, c. 2000BC. Seals of this kind, carved with carefully rendered animals and inscriptions in an undeciphered script, survive in considerable quantities. They were apparently used for commercial purposes.*

LEFT
*Silver roundel. Obtained at Rawalpindi, Punjab, Pakistan, c. 1st century AD. Such objects would have been sewn to clothing or leather and were probably decorative in function. Elephants and riders are reminiscent of the regal processions often represented in Indian sculpture.*

◄ INDUS CIVILISATION 2500–1500BC

LIFE OF THE BUDDHA 563–483BC

MAURYA 4TH CENTURY–230BC

1750BC    1500BC    1250BC    1000BC    750BC    500BC    250BC

Amaravati. Under the powerful Gupta rulers, who reunited the north of India between the third and fifth centuries, artistic schools at Mathura and Sarnath continued to produce Buddhist, Jain and Hindu images in stone, bronze and terracotta.

The Gupta era was brought to an end by invasions from Central Asia early in the sixth century. The ensuing period was marked by the construction of extravagant temples, handsomely endowed by local élites, and a wealth of regional styles evolved under the patronage of such dynasties as the Pallavas and Cholas in the south and the Calukyas in the Deccan.

With the arrival of Islam and the establishment of the Sultanate of Delhi in the late twelfth century, Islamic norms of behaviour were adopted in urban life, and Islamic conventions increasingly influenced the arts. Courtly life attained new heights of splendour under the Mughals, a Central Asian dynasty which controlled most of the north of India between the sixteenth and eighteenth centuries. This period saw a flowering of such decorative arts as jewellery, lapidary and manuscript painting.

Another outside influence was the presence of European traders and colonists who also began to arrive in the sixteenth century. Although by the mid-nineteenth century India had been absorbed into the British Empire, much of the subcontinent remained deeply traditional, and even in the present century there is a thriving popular art tradition based on ancient beliefs and practices.

BELOW

*Gold coin of Kanishka I, 2nd-3rd century AD. The face shows the Kushan king of Bactria and India. On the reverse is the Kushan version of the Iranian sun god Mithra. The Kushans extended the use of coins throughout Central Asia and northern India.*

RIGHT

*Miniature temple. From West India. Sandstone, 18th-19th century AD. Miniature temples, found at all the major Hindu religious sites in India, represent one way in which a person of humble means could contribute to a place of worship and pilgrimage.*

ABOVE

*Relief sculpture from Amaravati. Limestone, 3rd century AD. Part of the relief decoration from the Great Stupa at Amaravati which was founded in the 3rd century BC, possibly under the patronage of the great Mauryan emperor Asoka. An important focus of devotion for Buddhists, a stupa is a solid mound containing Buddha relics.*

| KUSHAN EMPIRE (N) SATAVAHANA (S) AD0-300 | GUPTA AD320-500 | | MEDIEVAL INDIAN DYNASTIES PRATIHARA AD600-950 • PALA AD750-1150 CHOLA AD900-1200 RASHTRAKUTA AD600-1000 | ISLAMIC INCURSIONS (AFGHANISTAN & CENTRAL ASIA) | | DELHI SULTANATE AD1199-1526 | | MOGHULS FROM CENTRAL ASIA • BABUR HUMAYUN • AKBAR JAHANGIR • AWRANGZEB | LATE MUGHAL PERIOD AD1707-1857 | DIRECT BRITISH RULE AD1857-1947 |
|---|---|---|---|---|---|---|---|---|---|---|
| | HUNA INVASION AD490-530 | | | | | | | | | |
| AD250 | AD500 | | AD750 | AD1000 | | AD1250 | | AD1500 | AD1750 | |

# JAPAN

JAPANESE CULTURE has often been influenced by that of mainland Asia, but this should not obscure the antiquity of its indigenous civilisation: indeed, the oldest datable pottery in the world is Japanese Jōmon ware from about 10,000BC. Organised agriculture arrived in the third century BC, and the ensuing Yayoi period (300BC–AD 300) saw the rapid adoption of technology from the mainland, including bronze and iron casting, weaving and the use of the potter's wheel. Society became more settled and class-based, bound together by observance of the nascent Shintō religion. During the Kofun period the power of local ruling families spread to bring political unity to the greater part of the islands.

Shintō, the 'way of the gods', was one of the strongest influences on the development of Japanese culture: with its emphasis on love and respect for the natural world, ancestors and craftsmanship, and on the inseparability of the physical and the spiritual, it played a large role in the adaptation and reinterpretation of ideas and techniques received from the mainland. Common Japanese stylistic traits, such as a fondness for and inventive use of asymmetry, were also applied to imported art forms such as lacquer with great success.

Buddhism first came to Japan in the sixth century AD, though it continued to evolve long afterwards under successive waves of influence from the mainland. Thus the intricate and formal court life of the Heian period (AD794–1185) was strongly coloured by the teachings of the Tantric Shingon school, while the samurai warrior class who controlled the country from 1185 to 1868 favoured the disciplined and introspective Zen tradition imported from China and Korea.

LEFT

*Haniwa. Low-fired red pottery, 6th century* AD. *The nobility of the Kofun period were buried in impressive stone chambered tombs covered by huge mounds of earth. Pottery figures (haniwa) in the form of people, animals, birds and houses were placed around the outer slopes of the mound.*

RIGHT

*Nō mask. Painted wood, 17th-18th century* AD. *The 500-year-old Nō masked theatre tradition continues to flourish, and the British Museum collections include masks donated by living mask carvers. This example represents the character of a young woman.*

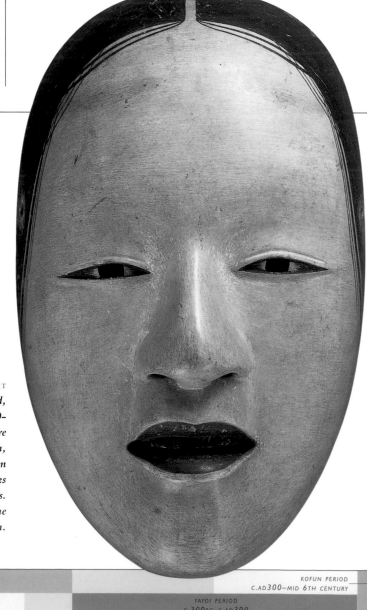

| JŌMON PERIOD C.10,000BC–C.300BC | | | | KOFUN PERIOD C.AD300–MID 6TH CENTURY |
|---|---|---|---|---|
| | | | YAYOI PERIOD C.300BC–C.AD300 | |

| 1000BC | 800BC | 600BC | 400BC | 200BC | 0 | AD200 |
|---|---|---|---|---|---|---|

28

With its emphasis on contemplation and intuitive thought and action, Zen translated religious philosophy into aesthetic activities such as calligraphy, ink painting, interior and garden design, martial arts and the tea ceremony with its distinctive pottery styles.

For over two hundred years, from about 1639, Japan was relatively isolated from external influences. This encouraged the creation or elaboration of indigenous styles: porcelain-production techniques were introduced in the early seventeenth century and native Japanese wares developed along very different lines from Chinese porcelains, both in style and function. From the 1660s, export porcelains were being produced for the European market.

The period of isolation was followed, from 1868, by a time of rapid and almost overwhelming Westernisation. However, the twentieth century has seen a revival of confidence in such traditional art forms as ceramics and calligraphy. There is also a flourishing school of Japanese-style painting (Nihonga), and Japanese prints, often very international in flavour, have a wide audience. Japan's rich regional traditions, including those of Okinawa and the Ainu in Hokkaidō, are now fully recognised.

ABOVE

*Lacquer writing box, 17th century AD. By the 12th century, Japanese lacquerers had surpassed their Chinese and Korean predecessors, and lacquer was widely used for domestic articles, furniture, ornaments and temple furnishings. From the 16th century, lacquerware was being produced for export and was avidly sought by Western collectors. The exquisite vignette on the inside of this writing box demonstrates the Japanese sense of overall design.*

RIGHT

*'Tiger' hanging scroll by Maruyama Ōkyo, AD1775. The hanging scroll format originated in the Heian period as a means of displaying Buddhist paintings, and was later adopted by Zen ink painters. By Ōkyo's time it had also become popular for purely secular subjects such as this tiger.*

| | | | | HEIAN PERIOD AD794–1185 | | MUROMACHI PERIOD AD1333–1568 | MOMOYAMA PERIOD AD1568–1600 | | MODERN PERIOD AD1868– |
|---|---|---|---|---|---|---|---|---|---|
| ASUKA PERIOD MID 6TH CENTURY–AD710 | | NARA PERIOD AD710–794 | | | KAMAKURA PERIOD AD1185–1333 | | | EDO PERIOD AD1600–1868 | |

| AD600 | AD800 | AD1000 | AD1200 | AD1400 | AD1600 | AD1800 |
|---|---|---|---|---|---|---|

# KOREA

THE KOREAN peninsula was already occupied in the Palaeolithic period; by Neolithic times its inhabitants were producing comb-patterned pottery. Its Bronze Age was characterised by the construction of large cist graves and dolmens, as well as the introduction of rice cultivation. The bronzes produced at this time are quite different from those of China and include ritual implements used in shamanic ceremonies.

By 400BC iron was being produced: considerable quantities of iron weapons and armour have been discovered in the south of the country. The high temperatures needed for iron production are associated with the emergence of stoneware pottery at this time. This period also saw the establishment of several Han Chinese colonies in the north. Korea was initially divided into four, but during the Three Kingdoms period (57BC–AD668) Kaya, in the central southern part of the peninsula, was absorbed into Silla in the south-east. Koguryo occupied the north and Paekche the south-west.

In Koguryo, stone tombs built in the form of stepped pyramids contained chambers decorated with wall paintings strongly influenced by those of Han China. Paekche had maritime contacts with south China, and also influenced the development of Buddhist art in Japan, where many of its artists and craftsmen emigrated. The dramatic stoneware funerary vessels produced in Kaya and Silla were probably used in shamanistic burial rituals. Silla tombs have also yielded spectacular sheet gold crowns, belts, shoes, earrings and vessels whose decoration possibly indicates an origin in the Scytho-Siberian steppe cultures of Central Asia.

Silla unified Korea in AD668; its splendid capital at Kyŏngju was based on the Tang Chinese capital at Chang-an. Close relations with China led to the introduction of a Chinese-style administration, and many Koreans travelled to China and beyond. The highly stratified society of the Unified Silla period persisted under the Koryŏ dynasty (918-1392), under whose rule the Buddhist Church grew both in

ABOVE

*Gold earrings. Three Kingdoms Period, 5th-7th century AD. Probably from a Silla royal tomb, there are few such pieces in Western collections.*

LEFT

*Illuminated manuscript of the Amitābha sūtra. Gold and silver paint on blue paper. Koryŏ dynasty, dated AD1341. The discourses of the Buddha are known as sutra, the commentaries on them abidharma and the rules of monastic conduct as vinaya. These comprise the three main branches of the Buddhist canon. The only illustration in this copy of the Amitābha sūtra, this painting shows the Buddha preaching.*

◀ NEOLITHIC 6000–1000BC

IRON AGE – PROTO THREE KINGDOMS 400BC–AD300

BRONZE AGE 1000–200BC

| 3000BC | 2500BC | 2000BC | 1500BC | 1000BC | 800BC | 600BC | 400BC | 200BC | 0 |
|---|---|---|---|---|---|---|---|---|---|

influence and wealth. Many fine works of art – paintings, illuminated manuscripts, sculptures and celadon wares – were produced for the glory of Buddhism.

Reproduction of the Buddhist scriptures was considered a meritorious act; in the eleventh century, the entire canon was printed from over 80,000 hand-carved woodblocks, an extraordinary accomplishment carried out in a vain attempt to protect Korea from invasion by the Mongols. The desire to print holy texts more quickly and efficiently led to the invention of movable metal type – the earliest in the world – in the early thirteenth century.

Buddhism was persecuted during the long Choson dynasty (1392-1910) when strict Confucianism was the prevailing philosophy. The fifteenth century, however, saw a flowering of science, technology and culture, though a series of Japanese invasions at the end of the sixteenth century caused great destruction. No sooner had Korea recovered from these incursions – sometimes called the 'Pottery Wars' because the Japanese took many potters as prisoners – than it was invaded by the Manchus, who were to form the Chinese Qing dynasty. However, the eighteenth century was a period of confident maturity which is reflected in the art of the time.

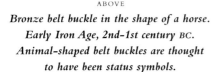

*ABOVE*

*Bronze belt buckle in the shape of a horse. Early Iron Age, 2nd-1st century BC. Animal-shaped belt buckles are thought to have been status symbols.*

*RIGHT*

*Water sprinkler (kundika). Porcelain with white slip inlay and celadon glaze. Koryŏ dynasty, 12th century AD. Water sprinklers like this were used in Buddhist rituals. The vessel shape originated in India and the technique of making translucent celadon glazes was imported from China, but the inlay technique was a Korean innovation.*

*ABOVE*

*Portrait of a Confucian scholar. Ink and colours on paper. Chosŏn dynasty, late 18th-19th century AD. The scholar is shown dressed in traditional white clothes and a hat made of woven horsehair. The detailed portrayal of the face shows the Western influence introduced via the Jesuit painters at the Chinese court in Beijing, which was visited by Korean painters and envoys.*

| | | | UNIFIED SILLA AD668–935 | | | | | JAPANESE OCCUPATION AD1910–1945 | |
| THREE KINGDOMS 57BC–AD668 | | | | KORYŎ AD918–1392 | | | | | |
| KOGURYO 37BC–AD668 | | | | | | | | | |
| PAEKCHE 18BC–AD663 | | | | | | | | | |
| KAYA AD42–562 | | | | | | | | CHOSŎN (YI) AD1392–1910 | |
| SILLA 57BC–AD668 | | | | | | | | | |

AD200    AD400    AD600    AD800    AD1000    AD1200    AD1400    AD1600    AD1800    AD2000

31

# OCEANIA

THE INHABITED ISLANDS of the Pacific region, collectively known as Oceania, can be divided into four groups: Melanesia, reaching from New Guinea to Fiji and including the Solomon Islands; Micronesia, the scattering of small islands to the north; Polynesia, the vast area stretching from Tonga in the east to Easter Island in the west, and from Hawaii in the north to New Zealand in the south; and the continent of Australia. Although this vast area of scattered islands encompasses an amazing diversity of cultures, most of its peoples grow food crops, while fishing remains important in coastal areas. The Aboriginal people of Australia, however, lived until recent times as hunter-gatherers.

Nowhere is the localised nature of Pacific society better seen than in Melanesia, the first area to be settled by the south-east Asian peoples who eventually populated the region. Here, even the largest island, New Guinea, is fragmented into tribal groups who often choose to emphasise their differences, regulating their co-existence by the exchange of gifts or oaths, by trade and by intermarriage. Their frequent feuds have given added importance to the manufacture of shields and weapons, which are often beautifully decorated.

Metal was unknown in the Pacific before the arrival of European explorers in the eighteenth century, but the Melanesians were skilled in crafting a variety of materials including wood, clay and shell, as can be seen from their elaborate architectural carvings and ritual masks. Boat building was another important industry, as warfare, trade and colonisation between the islands was entirely dependent on sea transport. The Solomon Islanders were especially skilled

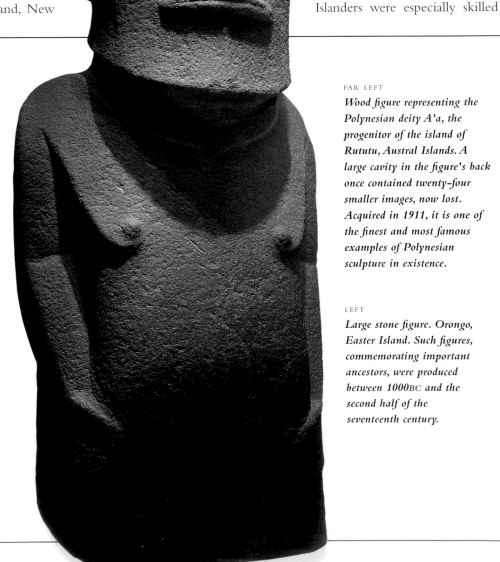

boatbuilders, constructing elegant black-painted canoes inlaid with intricate designs in white shell.

By the middle of the first millennium settlers had reached nearly all the islands of Micronesia and Polynesia. The cultivation of food crops such as taro, yams, breadfruit and coconuts was supplemented in places by the keeping of pigs and fishing. Societies could be complex, and among the larger islands, rank was often indicated by costume: in Hawaii, for example, chiefs wore cloaks and helmets covered in brightly coloured feathers. Sculpture was another important art form, typified by the monumental stone figures of Easter Island. Further south, the Maori culture of New Zealand is characterised by its sophisticated carvings in wood, stone and bone. In Australia, the complex religion and kinship networks of the Aborigines also found expression in paintings on rocks, bark and earth.

The arrival of the Europeans heralded enormous changes in the Pacific, although some traditional societies managed to remain untouched for many generations; the peoples of the central New Guinea Highlands, for example, avoided contact until the 1930s. Nonetheless, the cultural, religious and artistic interaction between Westerners and Pacific peoples has led to many interesting and productive developments in the arts and other areas.

LEFT

*Dress of the chief mourner. Tahiti. The dress is of barkcloth and the face-mask of pearl shell. Whole pearl shells decorate the wooden breast ornament, while the chest apron is made from pearl shell slivers. It was presented to Captain James Cook during his second voyage of 1772-5.*

RIGHT

*Mask. Saibai, Torres Strait Islands. Made of wood, with low-relief decoration, shell eyes and eyebrows and hair of vegetable fibre. Used in ceremonies associated with the ripening of the ubar fruit.*

ABOVE

*Nephrite neck pendant, hai tiki. Maori, New Zealand. Nephrite has always been highly prized by the Maori and was used extensively for prestigious weapons and personal ornaments. Such objects are treasured family heirlooms and are handed down from generation to generation, acquiring more spiritual power with each successive owner.*

# CENTRAL & SOUTH AMERICA

THE EARLIEST EVIDENCE of settled agricultural life in Central America dates from c. 3000–2000BC, but the first major civilisation, that of the Olmec, flourished around 1200BC. Olmec culture was characterised by large architectural complexes, monumental sculpture, fine lapidary work, pottery and the use of hieroglyphic writing, all traits that were assimilated by later civilisations, among them the Maya. Made wealthy by their highly successful farming methods, the great Maya city states were ruled by royal dynasties whose lineages, military exploits and kingly rituals were recorded in their sculptures and hieroglyphic inscriptions.

Elsewhere, other distinct traditions appeared. In the last centuries BC, the northern city of Teotihuacan emerged as a centre of religious and civic power. In the south the Zapotec flourished until around AD1200, when they were overthrown by the Mixtec, remarkable for their skills as architects, potters, lapidaries and goldsmiths.

By this late period much had changed across the region. On the Gulf Coast the Huastec people, probably a Maya-speaking group, had replaced the long-vanished Olmec and the Totonac who succeeded them. Their pyramids and sculptures and the deities they celebrated were markedly different from those of central Mexico, and evidence suggests that they had contact with the Aztec or Mexica of the central valleys, who were

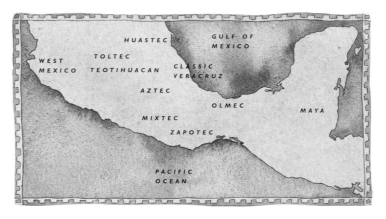

LEFT

*Votive jade axe. Olmec, 1200–400 BC. This massive ceremonial axe combines characteristics of the caiman and the jaguar, the most powerful predators of the tropical lowlands.*

ABOVE

*Carved stone lintel. From Yaxchilan, Mexico. Maya, AD770. One of a group of lintels carved to commemorate the accession to power of Lord Bird Jaguar. They illustrate the blood-letting rites performed in order to contact ancestral spirits (as shown here), ensure success in battle and obtain captives for sacrifice.*

OLMEC 1200–400BC
CHAVIN C. 1000–400BC

| 1200BC | 1000BC | 800BC | 600BC | 400BC | 200BC | 0 |

forging their own civilisation from the fourteenth century onwards.

By the early sixteenth century, the Aztec had risen by dynastic alliance, trade and conquest to dominate almost the entire region, incorporating regional gods into their own complex pantheon. As in all Central American cultures, Aztec life was dominated by religious, ceremonial and military power. This is illustrated by the magnificent masks and ritual objects fashioned from jade, turquoise, gold and other precious materials. By the time of the Spanish conquest in 1519-21, the Aztec capital Tenochtitlan had become the wealthiest and most powerful city in Central America.

There is some evidence of cultural exchange between Central and northern South America, especially in pottery forms and the use of metallurgy. The Andes and the fertile valleys which cut across the arid desert coast of Peru provided a dramatic backdrop for a succession of empires. Among the wealth of artistic production, the pottery portrait vessels made by the Mochica people of the Moché Valley and the elaborately patterned woven textiles of the Paracas region are outstanding. The peoples of Colombia and Peru also produced fine metalwork in gold, silver, copper and bronze: notably beautiful are the cast ornaments in the Quimbaya style of Colombia.

The Spanish destruction of the Inca empire and its capital Cuzco in 1534 signalled an abrupt end to an accomplished civilisation that once boasted an extraordinary road system and sophisticated engineering.

*Turquoise mosaic mask. Mixtec-Aztec, AD1400-1521. The Aztec royal court commissioned skilled Mixtec artisans to produce lapidary work of the highest order, notably mosaic masterpieces. A human skull forms the base for this mosaic mask of the creator-god Tezcatlipoca, 'Smoking Mirror'.*

RIGHT

*Limeflask made of tumbaga (a gold-copper alloy). Quimbaya style, AD400-900. The figure is hollow, with an opening on top of the head, and probably served as a container for lime powder which was taken while chewing coca leaves.*

ABOVE

*Pottery vessel. Mochica, late 6th-early 8th century AD. The ceramics of the Moché culture of coastal Peru were exceptionally sophisticated in both technique and design.*

| | | |
|---|---|---|
| MAYA 250BC AD1000 | | |
| TEOTIHUACAN 150BC–AD750 | HUASTEC AD900–1450 | |
| ZAPOTEC 200BC–AD800 | | |
| MOCHICA C. AD300–AD800 | | MIXTEC AD1200–1521 |
| | | AZTEC AD1300–1521 |
| NASCA 200BC–AD600 | ❖ QUIMBAYA C. AD1000 | INCA AD1438–1532 |

| AD400 | AD600 | AD800 | AD1000 | AD1200 | AD1400 | AD1600 |
|---|---|---|---|---|---|---|

35

# NORTH AMERICA

THE ORIGINAL PEOPLING of the Americas took place over 10,000 years ago, during the last Ice Age, when sea levels were lower than today and what is now the Bering Strait was a land-bridge linking the far north-west of America with Asia. Hunters in pursuit of mammoth and other large game crossed from Siberia into Alaska, from where they spread swiftly across both continents.

This rapid spread of population was accompanied by the development of specialised tools and lifestyles suited to the varied new environments of the Americas.

*Headdress of Yellow Calf. Eagle feathers, red trade cloth, glass beads, skin and horse hair. Arapaho, Wyoming, c.1900.*

Agriculture, for instance, developed over a thousand years ago, prompted by the intensive gathering of plants and the eventual arrival of seed-crops such as beans, maize and squash from Mexico. Farming and the establishment of long-distance trade routes encouraged the growth of distinct cultures such as the Adena and Hopewell peoples of the Ohio Valley, who constructed vast earthworks enclosing burial mounds containing rich grave goods.

Mesoamerican influence was even stronger later in southern areas of the United States such as the Mississippi region, home to an agricultural civilisation characterised by a distinctive pottery style and the construction of imposing ceremonial sites with flat-topped temple mounds and courts for ball games. In the south-west, a highly specialised farming culture developed to cope with the desert

*Ivory arrowshaft straightener, carved with two foetal caribou heads and engraved with scenes of dancing and hunting. Inupiaq, Alaska, c.1850.*

conditions; for the people of this region, the seasonal arrival of rain was and remains a matter of overwhelming importance, invoked to this day in song and ceremony, and depicted in art.

Throughout the continent, however, hunting remained an important source of food. In the space of the last millennium, the Inuit people of the northern coasts have specialised in the hunting of marine animals such as the seal, whale and walrus. This is reflected in their art, particularly the carved tools of bone and ivory. The introduction of the horse by the Spanish colonists of New Mexico enabled the peoples of the Plains to hunt bison more easily, providing them not only with food, but also with skins for clothes and shelters.

At the same time, the supply of furs to European traders became a staple economic activity, particularly in the north.

The first Europeans arrived in North America in the tenth century AD, but settlement did not begin in earnest until the sixteenth and seventeenth centuries. Drawn by the twin goals of preaching Christianity and exploiting the rich animal resources of the extensive forests, the settlers penetrated the continent along the great rivers of the east, bringing European diseases that decimated the native population.

During the nineteenth century, European Americans increasingly displaced the indigenous population, forcing them into reservations. Today, however, an increase in population among native Americans has been accompanied by cultural and political revival, best exemplified by the pow-wow.

BELOW
*Chilkat Tlingit blanket or cloak. Twined of mountain goat wool and cedar bark, with a crest, possibly a diving whale. Alaska, nineteenth century.*

ABOVE
*Stone smoking pipe in the form of a hawk eating a bird. Hopewell Culture, Mound City, Ohio, c. AD100-600. This was part of a cache of many hundreds of such pipes interred as a grave offering.*

ABOVE
*Hahay 'Iwuut', Kachina Mother/Pour water woman Kachina Doll. Hopi, Arizona, nineteenth century.*

# PREHISTORIC EUROPE

UMANS CAME to Europe about a million years ago, bringing with them the stone-working skills and hunter-gatherer lifestyle of their African ancestors. However, our own subspecies, *Homo sapiens sapiens*, did not arrive until about 40,000 years ago, during the last Ice Age. The ensuing period – the Upper Palaeolithic – saw not only technological advances in stone tools and weaponry but the appearance of art: delicate, stylised animal designs painted on cave walls or engraved on bone and flat pieces of stone.

As the polar icecaps retreated, an entirely different relationship with the natural world evolved. Agriculture, developed in the Middle East about 11,000 years ago, spread across Europe, reaching its western regions by 4000BC, and life became both more settled and more reliant on co-operation. New tools for working the land were created in stone and wood, and pottery vessels made to contain its produce.

As more complex societies emerged, eastern European art turned towards the representation of the human form, though the highly stylised examples surviving suggest super-human or ideal models rather than ordinary humans. In western regions large stone structures ranging from single standing stones to the imposing complex at Stonehenge began to be erected. The earliest trackways, built to assist the seasonal movements of herders, also date from this period.

Such improved communications also encouraged trade and helped bring the Neolithic period to an end as mining and metalworking, which began in the Balkans by 4000BC, spread across a large part of central Europe following the discovery of vast copper reserves. Alloyed with tin, copper produced bronze, an all-purpose alternative to stone that was swiftly adopted across the continent from 2500BC. The value and prestige of the new metal are obvious from the bronze weaponry found buried in hoards and graves all over Europe.

While literate and civilised societies grew up around the Mediterranean, the peoples of northern and central Europe

*'Bell' beaker. From Rudston, Yorkshire, c. 2200–1500* BC. *The placing of simple beaker-shaped vessels in graves was a widespread practice in western Europe during the Early Bronze Age.*

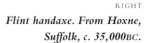

**Flint handaxe. From Hoxne, Suffolk, c. 35,000BC.**

◄ NEOLITHIC – BELL-BEAKER, BATTLE-AXE 6000–2000BC          LATER BRONZE AGE 1500–700BC

EARLIER BRONZE AGE 2000–1500BC

2250BC          2000BC          1750BC          1500BC

started to develop regional characteristics clearly exhibited in their grave goods. In the west, for example, a characteristic pottery vessel gave its name to the 'Beaker' culture, while eastern areas developed a type of pottery known as 'corded' ware from the patterns impressed on it by applying cords. In the later Bronze Age, however, some of these traditions declined: 'beakers', for instance, were replaced by a new range of pottery forms, and new local styles of design and decoration appeared. Gold, always valued as a more splendid alternative to bronze for decorative purposes, was cast or beaten into intricate shapes.

By the time that iron replaced bronze as the principal functional material in the first millennium BC, Europe was a patchwork of many warlike peoples whose names and identities are still unknown: instead, the two main phases of the northern Iron Age – Hallstatt and La Tène – are named after archaeological sites where typical artefacts of each period have been discovered in great numbers. In the La Tène period a highly abstract, and nowadays much admired, artistic style spread across much of Europe north of the Alps, an area noted for the construction of strongly defended hillforts and inhabited by structured warlike societies ruled over by wealthy princes. ▶

RIGHT
*Gold cup. From Rillaton, Cornwall, c. 1700–1400BC. One of only three examples known from temperate Europe, this prestigious vessel is made of sheet gold ribbed for added strength and decoration.*

RIGHT
*Neolithic trackway. Built of timber felled in 3806BC. The oldest trackway in Europe, constructed by Neolithic farmers to cross the marshy ground of the Somerset Levels.*

LEFT
*The Folkton Drums c. 2500–2000BC. These ornately carved solid chalk cylinders were found in a child's grave beneath a round barrow at Folkton, Yorkshire.*

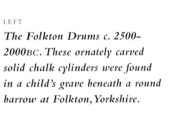

HALLSTATT B  800–700BC
HALLSTATT A  1100–800BC
IRON AGE – HALLSTATT C-D AND LA TÈNE  700BC–AD43

VILLANOVANS          ETRUSCANS

1000BC          750BC          500BC          250BC

# PREHISTORIC EUROPE

Among these peoples were those referred to as 'Celtic' by the Greeks and Romans, and it is this name (also given to certain languages spoken in modern times on the western coasts of the British isles and northern France) that is, somewhat misleadingly, applied to the last coherent European artistic tradition to predate the Roman conquest.

In Italy the Iron Age took a different turn, though areas of the north had strong affinities with 'Celtic' northern Europe. In the west of the peninsula and in the Po Valley the Proto-Etruscan culture showed early signs of urbanisation in the ninth century BC. Contact with Phoenician traders and the Greek colonists who settled in the south

and west from the eighth century introduced exotic imports from parts of the eastern Mediterranean, and as true cities grew up powerful local aristocracies emerged. The Etruscans, who wrote in an alphabet derived from Greek and buried their dead in magnificent tombs, were never united politically, but extended their influence north over the Apennines and south into Campania. The southern and central regions were peopled by many other tribal groups, among them those later known as Sabines, Samnites, Daunians and Peucetians.

LEFT

*Bronze flagon. From Basse-Yutz, France, c. 400BC. One of a pair decorated with inlays of coral and red enamel, this flagon is one of the outstanding examples of early 'Celtic' art of the La Tène period.*

BELOW

*The Great Torc. From Snettisham, Norfolk, 1st century BC. A characteristic 'Celtic' ornament, the torc is a heavy neck-ring made of twisted metal. This fine example is made of eight gold strands twisted together, each strand comprising eight gold wires. The ends are secured in elaborately decorated cast gold terminals.*

RIGHT

*Etruscan bronze mirror-back, c. 350–300BC. The engraving of legendary scenes on the backs of mirrors was one of the most highly developed forms of Etruscan art. This example shows the hero Perseus regarding the severed head of the gorgon Medusa.*

In Latium, to the south of the area inhabited by the Proto-Etruscans, a powerful city-dwelling people – the Latins – began to expand their power from the seventh and sixth centuries BC. Their greatest city, Rome, bequeathed their language and traditions to the next great empire of ancient Europe.

*The Battersea Shield. Found in the River Thames at Battersea, London, 1st century BC. This bronze facing from a wooden shield is decorated with flowing palmette and scroll designs enhanced with red enamel. The shield was probably deliberately consigned to the river as a ceremonial dedication to a 'Celtic' god.*

*Gold stater of Commius, c. 40–20 BC. Greek coinage was copied by the Iron Age peoples of central and northern Europe from the 3rd or 2nd century BC; by the mid-1st century the practice had spread to Britain. Commius was a king of the southern British tribe of the Atrebates.*

# THE GREEK WORLD

THE ANCIENT GREEK world occupied a large area of the eastern Mediterranean from the early Bronze Age to Roman times. In the later fourth millennium BC the Cycladic islands in the Aegean saw the birth of a distinctive culture producing simple marble figurines, fine stone vessels and painted pottery. During the later third and early second millennia the focus of Aegean civilisation shifted south to the Minoan culture of Crete, named after the island's legendary king Minos. Minoan wealth and prestige is evident in the architectural splendour of the palace at Knossos and in the fine Minoan jewellery, engraved gems and seals found throughout the Aegean.

In mainland Greece, a related civilisation at Mycenae and other sites of the Peloponnese survived into the late twelfth century BC.

ABOVE

*Silver tetradrachm coin of Athens, 450–406BC. The history of coinage has its origins in the Greek world of the early seventh century BC: the first metal coin was struck in the kingdom of Lydia in western Turkey around 625BC.*

The people of the Mycenean culture were linguistically related to the Greeks of later eras, and the linear script in which they kept their official accounts has been interpreted as an early form of Greek. The epics of Homer and other tales that later Greeks told of this period were written down long after reliable memories of it had faded.

For the Greek world the early Iron Age was an unsettled period of depopulation and migration. Later Iron Age pottery is charac-terised by striking geometric patterns, but by about 700BC figurative art was starting to return. Phoenician traders had already brought alphabetic writing to Greece; now, contact with the East reintroduced the Greeks to the art of human representation. Small bronze statuettes, larger marble figures possibly inspired by Egyptian models and vase paint-ing – first in black on a red background, then (from the late

LEFT

*Multiple hand-made vase from the island of Melos in the Cyclades. Early to middle Cycladic period, c. 2000BC.*

ABOVE

*The 'Master of the Animals', a Minoan gold pendant from the Aegina Treasure, c.1700–1500BC. The figure holds a water-fowl in each hand and is flanked by stylised plant-like elements.*

EARLY CYCLADIC I–III

EARLY MINOAN I–III

EARLY HELLADIC I–III

3000BC          2750BC          2500BC          2000BC

sixth century) red on black – all illustrate the development of the exploration of the human form as the central and most enduring aspect of Greek art.

Archaic Greece was a world of city-states interconnected by political and historical bonds such as those linking the many colonies of Italy, Sicily and Asia Minor to their mainland mother cities. These states were sometimes ruled by individual 'tyrants', who established themselves and their families as heads of government. More often, affairs were controlled by a small group of well-born men, or oligarchs. Elsewhere, decisions were made by the whole citizenry: all free, native, adult males. This was democracy, seen in its purest form at Athens in the mid-fifth century BC.

Democratic Athens is often regarded as typifying Greece's Classical age. The city's role in saving the mainland from conquest by Persia in 480BC and its acquisition of a wealthy Aegean empire, as recorded by the historian Thucydides, ensured Athens' political prominence until its defeat by Sparta in 404BC. Fifth-century Athens was a haven for philosophers, dramatists and artists such as Socrates and Aristophanes. This coincidence of imperial wealth and artistic splendour found brilliant expression in the Parthenon and other buildings of the Acropolis.

Elsewhere in the Greek world a variety of political systems coexisted. In Asia Minor these ranged from the kingship of local tyrants to the semi-independent rule ▶

LEFT
*Mycenean two-handled crater or jar, painted with a series of chariots, 1350-1325BC. Found in Cyprus where such Mycenean products were particularly popular.*

ABOVE
*Etruscan bronze helmet dedicated at Olympia. The inscription records the defeat of the Etruscans by the Syracusans under their tyrant, Hieron, in a sea battle in 474BC.*

| MIDDLE CYCLADIC I-III | | GEOMETRIC PERIOD | REFORMS OF CLEISTHENES, BIRTH OF DEMOCRACY 508BC ❖ |
|---|---|---|---|
| MIDDLE MINOAN I-III | LATE MINOAN I-III | | ARCHAIC PERIOD |
| MIDDLE HELLADIC | LATE HELLADIC | 776BC FIRST RECORDED ❖ OLYMPIC GAMES AT OLYMPIA | |
| 1500BC | 1250BC | 1000BC | 750BC |

# THE GREEK WORLD

established by the priests of powerful temples or sanctuaries. In Sicily, too, autocracy was the order of the day: in Syracuse the triumph of tyranny over democracy brought the city great power and influence over the whole island and much of southern Italy. Such regimes were often just as favourable to advances in philosophy, art and science as democracy had been: Syracuse provided a home for Plato, while his pupil Aristotle lived for some years in the little tyranny of Atarneus in Asia Minor. All along the Aegean coast, artists and architects created magnificent temples and

RIGHT

*Colossal statue of Maussolus. From the Mausoleum at Halicarnassus, 4th century BC. The Mausoleum was known in antiquity as one of the Seven Wonders of the World.*

tombs, such as the memorial built for Maussolus, ruler of the Carian city of Halicarnassus.

This diverse world was briefly unified in the fourth century BC, first by Philip of Macedonia, who forcibly united the states of the Greek mainland in 338, and then under his son Alexander the Great, who continued into Asia. In an astonishing campaign lasting eight years Alexander conquered Persia and gained control of a region stretching from Egypt to north-west India, thereby spreading Greek culture over a vast area.

The period between Alexander's death in 323BC and the Roman conquest of the Greek world is known as the Hellenistic era. Alexandria, the new Egyptian capital, acquired an unrivalled position as the capital of Hellenistic culture.

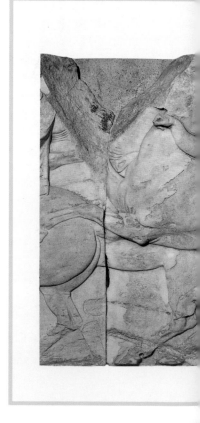

LEFT

*A woman-headed bird (or Siren) clutching a small human figure. From the 'Harpy Tomb' at Xanthos, Lycia, 470–460BC. In Greek myth and art Sirens helped to escort the dead to the Underworld and guarded their tombs.*

| ◀ 512–479BC PERSIAN INVASIONS OF GREEK MAINLAND | 480BC BATTLE OF SALAMIS, PERSIANS DEFEATED AT SEA 479BC BATTLE OF PLATAEA, PERSIANS DEFEATED ON LAND | 404BC ATHENS DEFEATED BY SPARTA | c. 350BC MAUSOLEUM OF HALICARNASSUS BUILT |
| 480BC ATHENS SACKED BY PERSIANS | PARTHENON CONSTRUCTED 447–432BC | CLASSICAL PERIOD | 323BC DEATH OF ALEXANDER THE GREAT |

| 450BC | 400BC | 350BC | 300BC |

However, the Hellenistic world was not blessed with peace. As the Macedonian empire dissolved, political supremacy in the Mediterranean and Near East was hotly contested by new superpowers, including Rome, a culture itself deeply influenced by Greece. Thus, although the fall of Egypt to the Romans in 31BC marked the end of Greek political independence in the Mediterranean, Greek thought, literature and art continued to be disseminated throughout the Roman and Byzantine empires into medieval times.

*Bronze head of a Berber. Found in the Temple of Apollo at Cyrene, c. 350–300BC. Greek colonies were established throughout the Mediterranean, including north Africa.*

*Athenian red-figure vase, 480–470BC, showing the scene from Homer's Odyssey in which the hero Odysseus is bound to the mast of his ship so that he can listen to the Sirens' songs without being enticed away.*

## THE PARTHENON SCULPTURES

Dedicated to Athena, the city's patron goddess, the Parthenon was the most important temple in ancient Athens. Built in the mid-fifth century BC, its architects were Ictinus and Callicrates and the famous sculptor Pheidias oversaw the carved decoration. Brought to England by Lord Elgin in the early nineteenth century, the sculptures are sometimes known as the Elgin Marbles. They include a large number of panels from the frieze that ran around the temple exterior, together with some fragmentary sculptures from the pediments and some of the metopes from the temple's south wall. The frieze, portraying a long procession of horsemen and votaries, has been interpreted as representing the Panathenaic festival, held every four years on the goddess' birthday.

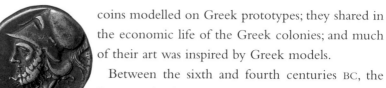

ACCORDING to legend, the city of Rome was founded by Romulus in 753BC. It was originally a monarchy, but its last king, an Etruscan, was ousted in 509BC, which marked the beginning of the Republic. Located in central Italy, surrounded by Etruscans, Sabines and Greek settlers, the Romans were exposed to a wide variety of outside influences from the earliest times. The Etruscan influence on Archaic Rome is clearly evident in its terracotta and cast bronze artwork, temple architecture and aristocratic, clan-based society. Another strong influence came from the Greek colonies in Sicily and southern Italy: the Romans worshipped many of the same gods as the Greeks; their alphabet derived from that of the Greeks; they struck

ABOVE

*Silver coin. Early Roman, c. 300BC. Contact with the Greek cities of Sicily and southern Italy led the early Romans to copy their coinage.*

coins modelled on Greek prototypes; they shared in the economic life of the Greek colonies; and much of their art was inspired by Greek models.

Between the sixth and fourth centuries BC, the Romans slowly extended their power base in Italy through conquest, treaty and alliance. From the third century, however, their horizons began to expand rapidly. The fall of the great naval power Carthage in 146BC following the lengthy Punic wars laid the foundations of Roman North Africa, later consolidated with the annexation of Egypt after the battle of Actium in 31BC. At the same time, further conquests in the eastern Mediterranean brought many former Greek territories under Roman rule.

Closer contact with the Greek world through the Greek slaves, hostages and merchants who came to Rome led to a second wave of Greek influence in philosophy, literature, religion and especially the

LEFT

*Bronze head of Augustus. From Meroë, 27–25BC. Coins and statues were the main media for propagating the emperor's image throughout the empire and a continuous reminder of Roman power.*

visual arts: most artists in the Roman world were Greeks or Near Easterners trained in Hellenistic traditions. Nonetheless, just as the bustle of Roman urban life, with its baths, theatres and gladiatorial shows, its aggressive electioneering and violent politics, was unique in the ancient world, so the Roman arts retained a distinct identity. Portrait sculpture, for instance, was especially developed, both on a grand scale, as in the life-sized statues of statesmen and generals, and in the humbler portraits found on private funerary monuments.

However, the Republic that achieved this unique blend of cultures eventually became a victim of its own success as its leaders' ambition grew. Finally, in 49BC, Julius Caesar defeated his rivals and became dictator; the resulting civil war led to the establishment of a monarchy, or 'Principate', under Augustus, Caesar's nephew and heir. By the time Augustus was declared emperor in 27 BC, Rome controlled the entire Mediterranean region, from Spain and Morocco in the west to Syria in the east. This culturally diverse empire was held together by the ▶

BELOW
*Funerary monument, 30-10BC. The subjects are a free-born Roman priest and his wife, a former slave. Among the privileges given by Augustus to freedmen and women was the right to marry Roman citizens.*

RIGHT
*Painted mummy portrait. From Hawara, Egypt, AD55-70. Realistic portraiture was a strong Roman tradition, and mummy portraits of the urban elite illustrate the fusion of different cultures that occurred in Egypt and throughout the empire.*

390BC GALLIC
LTS SACK ROME

EARLY ROMAN COINAGE
FROM C. 280BC

218–201BC SECOND PUNIC WAR WITH CARTHAGINIANS.
HANNIBAL INVADES ITALY AND NEARLY CONQUERS ROME

CAESAR'S CONQUEST OF
CONTINENTAL GAUL 58-51BC

AUGUSTUS DECLARED EMPEROR.
BEGINNING OF THE EMPIRE 27BC

312BC ROME'S FIRST MAJOR ROAD
BUILT IN ITALY, THE VIA APPIA

290BC ROME CONTROLS
ALL OF CENTRAL ITALY

146BC CARTHAGE AND
CORINTH DESTROYED

EXPEDITIONS TO BRITAIN
55–54BC

JULIUS CAESAR
MURDERED 44BC

400BC      300BC      200BC      100BC      0

47

# THE ROMAN EMPIRE

## THE ROMAN ARMY

The *pax Romana* – the peace that existed throughout the vast Roman empire in the first and second centuries AD – was largely dependent on the efficient army that protected its borders. Recruited from throughout the empire, soldiers were organised into legions comprising three to six thousand infantrymen supported by cavalry, military engineers, craftsmen and administrators.

Their commanding generals were more often career politicians than professional soldiers. When not on campaign, soldiers were based in forts. The letters and artefacts recovered from the fort at Vindolanda, near Hadrian's Wall, provide vivid insights into the daily lives of the foreign soldiers garrisoned there. This letter from a Roman soldier at the fort is written in ink on a wooden tablet.

figure of the emperor: religion, poetry, sculpture, even the writing of history, all reflected his central role.

Britain was the northernmost outpost of the empire. Its conquest began in AD43, and the south of the country was soon thoroughly Romanised. Urban centres such as London, Gloucester, Bath and *Verulamium* (St Albans) provided many of the comforts of Rome, while the countryside was dotted with the country estates and villas of the wealthy. However, the island was never wholly subdued, and remained a heavily militarised frontier province. In the second century AD both Hadrian and Antoninus Pius built great walls in the north, not simply as barriers against hostilities, but also as a means of imposing order on the surrounding area.

The third century was a period of turmoil, during which a long series of civil wars and disasters on its frontiers led to great instability within the empire. Reunited under Diocletian at the end of the century, Rome recovered its strength under the emperor Constantine. In AD313, with the Edict of Milan, Constantine

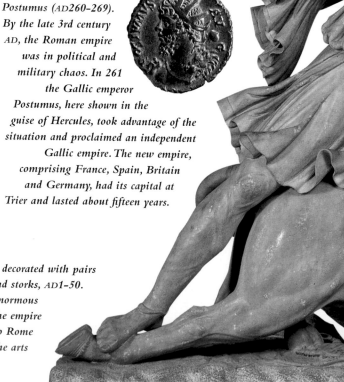

RIGHT

*Coin portrait of Postumus (AD260-269). By the late 3rd century AD, the Roman empire was in political and military chaos. In 261 the Gallic emperor Postumus, here shown in the guise of Hercules, took advantage of the situation and proclaimed an independent Gallic empire. The new empire, comprising France, Spain, Britain and Germany, had its capital at Trier and lasted about fifteen years.*

LEFT

*Silver bowl decorated with pairs of cranes and storks, AD1–50. With the enormous wealth of the empire flowing into Rome and Italy, the arts flourished.*

| | | | |
|---|---|---|---|
| JULIO-CLAUDIAN DYNASTY AD27–68 | ❖ POMPEII AND HERCULANEUM BURIED DURING ERUPTION OF VESUVIUS AD79 | ANTONINE EMPERORS AD117–193 | |
| ❖ ROMAN OCCUPATION OF BRITAIN AD43 ❖ | FLAVIO-TRAJANIC DYNASTY AD69–117 ❖ HADRIAN'S WALL BEGUN C. AD122 | | SEVERAN EMPERORS AD193–235 |
| AD50 | AD100 | AD150 | AD200 |

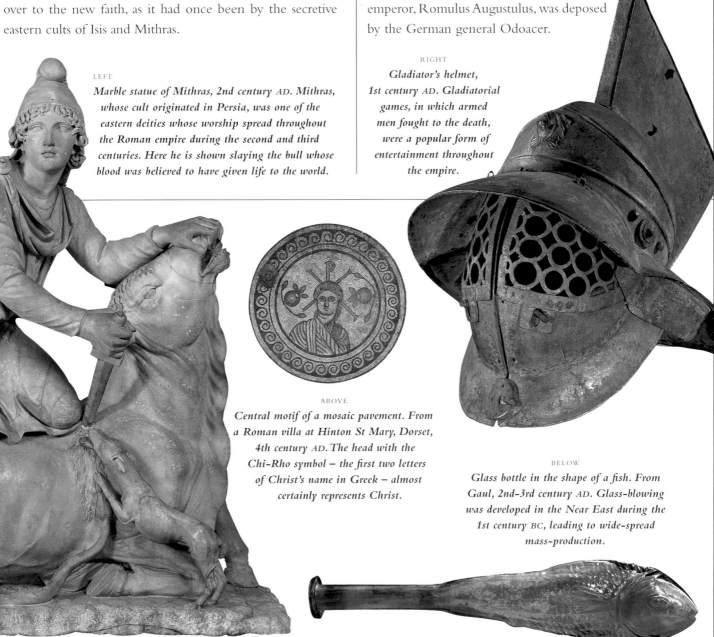

ROMAN EMPIRE IN SECOND CENTURY AD

ANTONINE WALL

BRITAIN

GAUL

SPAIN

ITALY GREECE
ROME

TURKEY SYRIA
ATHENS
CYPRUS

CARTHAGE

TUNISIA

EGYPT

changed the position of the Christian church overnight through his official recognition of Christianity. Formerly suppressed, it now became one of the pillars of state, and aristocrats and officials rushed to profess its teachings. Christian symbolism appeared on silverware, mosaics and pottery, although scenes and images from the pagan legends long embedded in the popular imagination were never completely ousted. The army, too, was eventually won over to the new faith, as it had once been by the secretive eastern cults of Isis and Mithras.

Since the end of the third century, the eastern and western halves of the empire had been administered separately. In 330 Constantine moved his seat of government east to Constantinople, which survived as the capital of the Byzantine empire for another thousand years. In the west, however, Rome was increasingly unable to cope with the pressure of invasions by Franks, Goths and Vandals. Finally, in 476, the last emperor, Romulus Augustulus, was deposed by the German general Odoacer.

LEFT

*Marble statue of Mithras, 2nd century AD. Mithras, whose cult originated in Persia, was one of the eastern deities whose worship spread throughout the Roman empire during the second and third centuries. Here he is shown slaying the bull whose blood was believed to have given life to the world.*

RIGHT

*Gladiator's helmet, 1st century AD. Gladiatorial games, in which armed men fought to the death, were a popular form of entertainment throughout the empire.*

ABOVE

*Central motif of a mosaic pavement. From a Roman villa at Hinton St Mary, Dorset, 4th century AD. The head with the Chi-Rho symbol – the first two letters of Christ's name in Greek – almost certainly represents Christ.*

BELOW

*Glass bottle in the shape of a fish. From Gaul, 2nd–3rd century AD. Glass-blowing was developed in the Near East during the 1st century BC, leading to wide-spread mass-production.*

ROMAN CITIZENSHIP EXTENDED TO ALL FREE INHABITANTS OF THE PROVINCES AD212 ❖ INITIAL DIVISION OF EMPIRE UNDER DIOCLETIAN AD286 ❖ FINAL DIVISION OF THE EMPIRE INTO EAST AND WEST AD395

SACK OF ROME BY VISIGOTHS AD410 ❖ DEPOSITION OF THE LAST ROMAN EMPEROR OF THE WEST AD476

FREEDOM OF CHRISTIAN WORSHIP RECOGNISED UNDER CONSTANTINE AD313 ❖ CONSTANTINOPLE CONSECRATED AS NEW IMPERIAL CAPITAL AD330

AD250    AD300    AD350    AD400    AD450

# MEDIEVAL EUROPE

FOLLOWING THE collapse of the Roman empire in the fifth century AD, local ruling classes throughout the provinces were left to themselves to protect their Romanised lifestyle from the threats of barbarian invasions and internal discord. One area where a Romanised aristocracy did survive relatively undisturbed was in eastern Europe, where the Byzantine empire held sway for another thousand years. In the west, however, local 'Romans' faced a troubled future. One approach they adopted was to enlist aid from the barbarians themselves: in Britain, for example, Anglo-Saxon peoples first arrived as mercenaries, though they soon established their own kingdoms, much as other Germanic peoples were doing in France and Italy.

Under the patronage of these new rulers, Germanic artistic traditions were combined with classical elements to produce the spectacular jewels and weaponry found in wealthy graves such as the seventh-century Sutton Hoo ship burial. Although the conversion of pagan kings to Christianity ended the practice of burying artefacts with the dead, it helped to reunite western Europe, paving the way for a revival of learning in the early ninth century.

By the eleventh century, trade and warfare had led to the consolidation of large kingdoms in western Europe. Already Viking seafarers from the north had been active from the Baltic to the Mediterranean. Although their intrusions into

LEFT

*Byzantine ivory carving. From Constantinople, 6th century AD. One leaf of an ivory diptych, this carving of the Archangel Michael illustrates the persistence of Greek and Roman traditions in Byzantine art.*

## THE SUTTON HOO SHIP BURIAL

In 1939 a great barrow excavated at Sutton Hoo in Suffolk yielded a remarkable find: a rich Anglo-Saxon burial contained within the hull of a long ship. Among the treasures were large quantities of gold, jewellery and functional items such as weaponry, buckets and a musical instrument. Dated to the seventh century by coins, the burial seems to be that of a local ruler, possibly Redwald, king of the East Angles and overlord of the Anglo-Saxon kingdoms, who died c. AD625. The most spectacular finds included this magnificent iron helmet and a pair of gold shoulder clasps inlaid with garnet and coloured glass.

mainland Europe were often brief and destructive, Viking settlements in Britain and Ireland stimulated the growth of trade and urban development. Scandinavia, for the first time, was brought into the sphere of Europe.

As the European nations crystallised, common artistic styles developed. Romanesque architecture, typified by round, classically inspired arches and barrel-vaulted ceilings, was adopted for churches and monastic buildings in both northern and southern Europe from the ninth to the twelfth century. The subsequent rise of French power in the thirteenth century coincided with a general trend towards the Gothic style, characterised by pointed arches, rib-vaulted ceilings and more slender proportions. The great Gothic cathedrals of northern Europe well illustrate the new emphasis on ambitious artistic endeavours, although smaller-scale artistic achievements in such disciplines as enamelwork and ivory carving are equally eloquent.

The deep religious feeling expressed in the art of medieval Europe culminated between the eleventh and thirteenth centuries in the Crusades, a series of military expeditions aimed at recapturing Christian holy places in the Near East from Islamic control. However, the chief effect of the Crusades was to diminish Byzantine power in the region, ultimately leading to the fall of Constantinople in the fifteenth century.

LEFT

*The Londesborough Brooch. Silver gilt set with amber, Irish, mid to late 8th century AD. One of the finest brooches in the British Museum's medieval collection. Rich enough to have belonged to a king or to a church treasury, its history is unknown beyond inclusion in Lord Londesborough's collection.*

RIGHT

*The Royal Gold Cup. Enamelled gold, c. AD1380. A masterpiece of French Gothic art, the Royal Gold Cup was originally made as a gift for Charles V of France, but formed part of the English royal collections in the 15th and 16th centuries. The decoration shows scenes from the life of St Agnes.*

BELOW

*Romanesque gilt copper and enamel altar cross. Mosan, c. AD1160, reset in the sixteenth century.*

FIRST CRUSADE TAKES JERUSALEM 1099 ❖    BUILDING OF CHARTRES CATHEDRAL 1194 ❖

❖ BATTLE OF HASTINGS 1066    FOURTH CRUSADE TAKES ❖
CONSTANTINOPLE 1204

AD900    AD950    AD1000    AD1050    AD1100    AD1150    AD1200

THE PERIOD extending from the fourteenth century until the death of Michelangelo in 1564 has been termed the Renaissance, when a renewed emphasis on classical learning was employed as the basis for a humanist interpretation of the universe. Its principles were keenly manifested in the arts of Italy, where Vasari's *Lives of the Most Excellent Painters, Sculptors and Architects* (1550) was the key work in establishing a critical framework for the development of European art, reflecting a new status for the artists themselves. Dürer was a vital point of contact between the culture of northern and southern Europe after his two journeys to Italy of 1494–5 and 1505–7, achieving a personal renown that was symptomatic of the changing status of artists.

The Reformation and diffusion of Protestantism in the north had pro

ABOVE

*Cast bronze medal of Leon Battista Alberti (1404–1472) by Matteo de' Pasti (fl. c. 1441–68). One of the foremost scholars of the Renaissance, Alberti was the author of treatises on painting, sculpture and architecture.*

found implications for religious imagery, taking advantage of the introduction of the printed medium for the propagation of its ideas. Successive waves of religious persecution brought about the exile of many important groups of craftsmen; the Protestant Huguenots, for example, were driven out of France and settled in England from the mid-sixteenth century, including gold and silversmiths, miniature painters, and ivory carvers.

The continuing importance of classical knowledge lay behind the phenomenon of the Grand Tour, an indispensable part of the education of the British aristocracy from the early seventeenth century. Their patronage resulted in the importation of countless antiquities, Old Master paintings, prints and drawings as well as contributing to the growth of

RIGHT

*'Ideal head of a woman' by the sculptor, painter, architect and poet Michelangelo Buonarroti (1475–1564). This highly finished drawing, dated to the second half of the 1520s, was intended as a work of art in its own right to be presented to a patron or close friend.*

LEFT

*'Nemesis' or 'The Great Fortune' by Albrecht Dürer (1471–1528), 1501–2. The central figure of 'Nemesis' in this engraving is based on the canon of proportions derived from Vitruvius' classical treatise on architecture, a seminal text for the Renaissance.*

RIGHT

*Maiolica (tin-glazed earthenware) bowl by Nicole da Urbino d. 1537/8. Painted c. 1524, this bowl is one of a set made for the outstanding patron and collector Isabella d'Este, whose arms and personal devices appear at the centre.*

| ❖ BRUNELLESCHI ADDS DOME TO FLORENCE CATHEDRAL 1420 | ❖ FIRST PRINTED BOOK: MAINZ PSALTER 1457 | ❖ BRAMANTE REBUILDS ST PETER'S, ROME 1506 | PALLADIO PUBLISHES FOUR BOOKS OF ARCHITECTURE 1570 |
| --- | --- | --- | --- |
| | | ❖ LUTHER PUBLISHES HIS 95 THESES 1517 | |
| | COLUMBUS'S FIRST VOYAGE TO AMERICA 1492 ❖ | ❖ MICHELANGELO PAINTS | BIRTH OF |
| FALL OF CONSTANTINOPLE 1453 ❖ | | SISTINE CHAPEL, ROME 1508-41 | SHAKESPEARE 1564 ❖ |

| AD 1400 | AD 1425 | AD 1450 | AD 1475 | AD 1500 | AD 1525 | AD 1550 |

52

Rome and Naples as major artistic centres by the latter part of the eighteenth century. By this stage the legacy of antiquity, stimulated by new archaeological discoveries, was playing a dynamic role in the evolution of a neo-classical style epitomised by the ceramic wares of Josiah Wedgwood; he derived much inspiration from the Greek vase collection that the British Museum purchased in 1772 from Sir William Hamilton, the British envoy in Naples.

In contrast with the decorum of Neoclassicism was the Romantic emphasis on the sublime effects to be drawn from the relationship between man and nature. The early manifestations of the Industrial Revolution combined with the

NEC SPE.
NEC METV.

START OF THIRTY YEARS' WAR ❖
IN GERMANY 1618

LAST OTTOMAN ATTACK ON VIENNA 1683 ❖

FOUNDATION OF BRITISH MUSEUM 1753 ❖

❖ NEWTON PUBLISHES PRINCIPIA MATHEMATICA 1687

AD 1600          AD 1625          AD 1650          AD 1675          AD 1700          AD 1725          AD 1750

53

political upheavals of the end of the late eighteenth and early nineteenth centuries to engender a mood of apocalyptic fervour that informed so much of the work of the visionary artist and poet William Blake.

The Napoleonic Wars helped to crystallise nationalist feeling, which gathered momentum throughout Europe in the course of the nineteenth century. In artistic terms this was often expressed through historical revivalism; for example, the neo-Grecian building designed by Robert Smirke for the British Museum was itself linked to a belief that Athens was the cradle of democracy whose legacy was embodied in the British political system. On the other hand, Gothic Revivalism, whose most brilliant exponent in Britain was A.W. N. Pugin, was the style chosen for the design and decoration of the new Houses of Parliament that opened in 1847, because it evoked the spiritual values of the Christian Middle Ages.

ABOVE

*Plate from 'The Song of Los', 1795, by William Blake (1757-1827). Throughout the early 1790s Blake was working on the printing of both text and images for a group of prophetic books, entirely of his own invention. The struggle of the creative spirit to survive in the material world is symbolised here by the oppressive figure with his hammer atop a fiery globe.*

LEFT

*Sir Isaac Newton (1642-1727) by David Le Marchand (1674-1726). The English mathematician, physicist, astronomer and philosopher Newton personified the spirit of scientific enquiry that characterised the Age of Enlightenment. This ivory bust was carved from life by Le Marchand, a Huguenot ivory carver, in 1718.*

## THE SPIRIT OF INQUIRY

One of the aspects of the spirit of inquiry fostered by the Renaissance was the desire to provide a systematic classification of all areas of knowledge. This eventually extended to the arrangement of many of the collections that were later absorbed into Europe's major museums. Foremost amongst these was the British Museum, which was founded by Act of Parliament in 1753 to house the collections of Sir Hans Sloane (1660-1753). A physician by profession, his lucrative practice enabled him to indulge his great passion for natural science and collecting. He became a Fellow of the Royal Society in 1685, and in 1727 its President in succession to Newton. On his death, he left (in addition to a library and a herbarium) some 80,000 objects, which included 'things relating to the customs of ancient times or antiquities', coins and medals, and books, prints and manuscripts. The same impulse to expand the frontiers of knowledge, allied to the mercantilism of the European courts, supplied the incentive for geographical exploration; the establishment of additional trade routes and contact with hitherto unknown continents introduced new materials and imagery that had an immediate impact on European culture.

LEFT

*The Pegasus Vase was presented by Wedgwood to the British Museum in 1786 as a supreme example of the quality of work produced at his pottery, Etruria, in Staffordshire. The main motif, dubbed 'The Apotheosis of Homer', was based on a drawing from an Athenian red-figure vase that formed part of the Hamilton collection.*

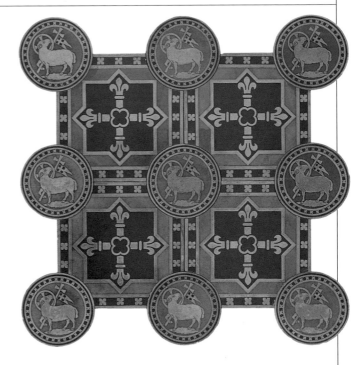

ABOVE

*Tile panel from the floor of the Roman Catholic Cathedral of St George in Southwark, London, built between 1841 and 1848. Designed by the cathedral's architect, A. W. N. Pugin, and manufactured by Minton & Co., the floor incorporates medieval motifs within a highly original design and colour scheme.*

55

# MODERN EUROPE

URING THE COURSE of the nineteenth century the concept of modernity became inseparable from the development of an industrialised urban consumer society, whose advent was most notably proclaimed by the Great Exhibition of 1851 at the Crystal Palace in London. It was impossible for artists, designers or educators to maintain a neutral stance towards the means of production, giving rise on the one hand to a desire to harness the principles of good taste to the processes of mass production and on the other to the Ruskinian belief in the moral and artistic superiority of handicraft. One of the most innovative designers of the late nineteenth century was a professor of botany, Christopher Dresser, who achieved considerable individuality of expression in all branches of the applied arts, exploiting new technology with particular success in his metalwork designs. He firmly rejected a Eurocentric historicism in favour of a variety of Japanese, South American and Islamic influences, working with both organic and geometric forms.

Charles Rennie Mackintosh, the architect of the Glasgow School of Art, introduced new structural principles into the design of his buildings and their related fittings, which contributed to the evolution of an international modernist style. However, Mackintosh was not concerned with the democratisation of design through collaboration with industrial manufacture. This issue was addressed in Germany by the activities of the Deutsche Werkbund founded in 1907, later by the Bauhaus founded in 1919, and in Scandinavia whose domestic products became a byword for high calibre design that catered for a broad market.

In the fine arts modernism was allied to the weakening of academic authority and the desire for new forms of expression that would articulate contemporary life. The French Impressionist painters who exhibited as a group between 1874 and 1886 liberated the whole field of artistic endeavour, shifting the emphasis away from the sanction of tradition in favour of the perpetual re-invention of an avant-garde identity. In the twentieth century there is no

RIGHT

*From autumn 1906 until the following summer Picasso (1881-1973) was immersed in the many studies leading up to the controversial painting 'Les Demoiselles d'Avignon', the 'cornerstone of modern art'. In the form in which Picasso finally left it, the composition contained five female figures, including one related to this figure executed in the winter of 1906-7.*

LEFT

*Oak clock with stencilled black decoration. Designed by C.R. Mackintosh (1868-1928) in 1919 for the guest bedroom of the house of the engineering-model manufacturer W.J. Bassett-Lowke in Northampton.*

❖ GREAT EXHIBITION, ❖ DARWIN PUBLISHES ORIGIN OF SPECIES 1859    DEATH OF QUEEN VICTORIA 1901 ❖    ❖ FOUNDING OF DEUTSCHE
LONDON 1851      WERKBUND 1907
BRITISH MUSEUM BUILDING      FIRST WORLD WAR 1914-18 ❖
COMPLETED 1850 ❖     ❖ FRANCO-PRUSSIAN WAR 1870    PICASSO PAINTS 'LES DEMOISELLES D'AVIGNON' 1907 ❖

AD 1850     AD 1860     AD 1870     AD 1880     AD 1890     AD 1900     AD 1910

56

more brilliant example of the capacity for constant renewal than the career of Picasso as painter, draughtsman, print-maker and sculptor whose influence has been universal.

Expressionism, which developed in Germany in the first decade of the twentieth century, provided a highly charged vocabulary that was especially appropriate to conveying the sense of dislocation and trauma created by the First World War and its aftermath. By the early 1920s Expressionism had lost its appeal for the more radical artistic factions; they turned variously to devising anti-rational visual languages such as Dadaism and Surrealism, or to the rigorously com-posed elements of Constructivism which the Bauhaus teacher Moholy-Nagy described as 'fundamentals that are without deceit...the socialism of vision'.

The latter part of Moholy-Nagy's career, like that of so many émigrés from Germany and Eastern Europe, lay in America, which became the major beneficiary of pro-gressive developments in Europe between the Wars. With its exciting industrial and urban imagery and vast domestic market for consumer goods, the United States had long pro-vided fertile ground for designers, artists and theoreticians. One of the most influential tracts of 'Americanism' was the historical study *Mechanization Takes Command* published in 1948 by the Swiss author Siegfried Giedion, which became a seminal text in Britain for artists like Richard Hamilton and Eduardo Paolozzi. At the same time the assimilation of Cubism, Surrealism and the pure abstraction of artists like the Bavarian-born Hans Hofmann or the Dutchman Piet Mondrian laid the groundwork for a quintessentially American movement, Abstract Expressionism.

From the mid-1960s a more assertive European identity emerged, coupled with a greater eclecticism in art and design in both the United States and elsewhere that has acknowledged the increasing pluralism of cultural reference in our global society.

*The portfolio of lithographs that Moholy-Nagy (1895-1946) executed in 1923 remains one of the purest expressions of Constructivist values in the field of original printmaking. His principal interests lay in photographic experimentation and typographical and industrial design.*

*One of the first coffee percolators in fireproof glass. The design evolved over the period 1925-30 as the outcome of a collaboration between Gerhard Marcks (1889-1974), artistic director of the Bauhaus Pottery Workshop from 1919 to 1925, and the manufacturer Schott & Genossen in Jena, Germany.*

*The American Norman Bel Geddes (1893-1958) set up his own firm in 1927, specialising in streamlined designs for trains, cars and aeroplanes as well as some small-scale household items. This medal was struck in silver for the 25th anniversary of General Motors in 1933.*

SECOND WORLD WAR 1939-45　　　FIRST MOON LANDING 1969　　　COLLAPSE OF BERLIN WALL 1989

AD 1930　　　AD 1940　　　AD 1950　　　AD 1960　　　AD 1970　　　AD 1980　　　AD 1990

# CONSERVATION

IT IS NOT GOOD enough for museums to collect, document, research, store and display fascinating objects: they must do all they can to prevent them decaying further. The use of the word 'further' is deliberate, because it is a law of nature that every object starts to decay from the moment it is produced. But efforts can be made to slow down the rate of decay, and it is the function of museum conservation departments to do this. There are two basic ways in which this can be achieved, either by direct intervention on objects ('active conservation') or by providing the best possible environment so that decay processes are reduced to a realistic minimum ('passive conservation').

Conservation was practised in one form or other from the earliest days at the British Museum. The earliest practitioners were craftsmen trained to make and restore objects. The need for special methods came to a focus in 1845 when the Portland Vase was smashed into 200 pieces in an act of vandalism. A museum craftsman, Mr Doubleday, was given the task of repairing the vase, and he did an excellent job, it being necessary to repeat the task only in 1948 and then again in 1989. These three dates are of interest in that they represent different phases in the state of conservation attitudes and techniques. In 1845 there were no specialists and Doubleday was untrained. By 1948 there were 'craftsmen restorers' working as professionals but no vocational courses were available and they learned their skills at the bench. There are no records of how the Portland Vase was conserved in 1845 or 1948. In 1989 the whole process was closely documented and a film was made of the process. By this time all conservators received specialist training and were working within a Department of Conservation, set up in 1975. Some conservators need to be very highly specialised. There are specialist conservators for cuneiform tablets, coins and papyrus for instance.

All objects in permanent and temporary exhibitions are examined prior to display by conservators, who ensure that they are stable enough for their life inside glass cases. The materials from which cases are constructed and decorated

ABOVE

*Nigel Williams conserving the Portland Vase in 1989. Because the adhesive used in the previous restoration was deteriorating, the vase was dismantled into its 200 or so separate pieces and reassembled using the most modern adhesives.*

RIGHT

*John Doubleday sits beside the restored Portland Vase. On the left is a watercolour of the vase in pieces, made shortly after its near destruction in 1845.*

58

have to be tested to ensure they they are not themselves the source of unacceptable pollution. The galleries have to be checked to make sure that the light levels are not too high, causing colours to fade and objects to fall apart. The atmosphere itself must not create dangers, and humidity, temperature, dust levels and pollution are measured, and can now be monitored remotely. Not infrequently, British Museum conservators are assigned to archaeological excavations, when on-site conservation may be vital for the survival of newly discovered objects.

The processes of conservation are demanding, but the British Museum has a responsibility to ensure that objects are not only available for our own generation, but for hundreds of years to come.

RIGHT
*Working in a very restricted space at the bottom of a deep grave shaft, a British Museum conservator, Pippa Cruickshank, is involved with consolidating and lifting friable organic material. Khirbet Qazone Excavation, Jordan, 1997.*

ABOVE
*A humidity gauge is checked in an exhibition gallery.*

LEFT
*A recently conserved Chinese painting. Wang.E (fl. late 15th–early 16th century), ink and pale colours on silk.*

# SCIENTIFIC RESEARCH

I T COMES AS A surprise to some to discover that the British Museum supports several scientific laboratories containing state-of-the-art equipment and staffed by research scientists. The research programmes are directed entirely to the better understanding of collections, complementing more traditional curatorial studies, and can lead to fundamental reassessment of received opinion. In many ways the Museum has always been a scientific institution: the first director, Gowin Knight, was a fellow of the Royal Society and he established his personal magnetical laboratory in Montagu House, the Museum's first home, in the late 1750s.

Scientific analyses of artefacts in museums started at least as early as

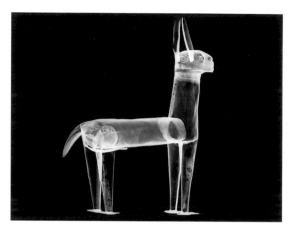

ABOVE
*Radiograph of a Pre-Columbian llama from Peru, showing its construction from sheet gold components soldered together.*

the 1850s in Great Britain. Until 1880 the British Museum at Bloomsbury was a science museum in the sense that it possessed the nation's collections of botany, zoology and mineralogy specimens, and the earliest chemical analysis of artefacts was conducted by scientists in the Mineral Department on metal objects from Cyprus. What is of particular interest is that this work was commissioned by the greatest antiquities curator of his day, Augustus Wollaston Franks.

A research group dedicated to the use of scientific techniques was established for the first time in 1920 when Alexander Scott, of the government's Department of Scientific and Industrial Research, was seconded to the Museum to investigate the condition of objects

ABOVE
*Xero-radiograph of the sword, as excavated in 1991, from the Sutton Hoo ship burial. It shows a buckle and, below it, a pyramid mount within the associated soil and corrosion.*

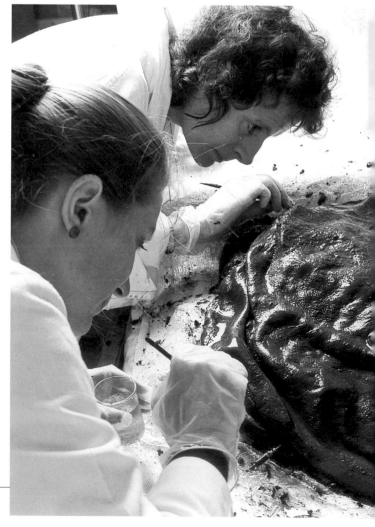

which had suffered in emergency storage during the First World War. Most of the work of the original Research Laboratory was to do with conservation, but Dr Scott, like Franks before him, saw the potential of science in solving much wider questions about the past.

Some of the equipment, for example, can accurately measure the amounts of the different substances from which objects are made. Some of these substances, even though occurring in very small amounts, can be diagnostic of the source of the raw materials used in the manufacturing processes, thereby contributing to the understanding of trade routes and trade relationships in the past. When metal objects which purport to be old are composed of very pure components, suspicions may be aroused as early purification techniques were not as efficient as today's. Fakes have not infrequently been identified in this way. Even material that is apparently unprepos-

ABOVE

*A zinc-smelting furnace dating to the 14th century AD, at Zawar, Rajasthan, India, with some of the retorts, which contained ore and reducing agents, still in situ.*

sessing, such as metallurgical debris, can provide information about early technology, as can the objects themselves. In this, radiography is an indispensable tool providing information about the interior of objects and thus their structure without any destructive sampling or sectioning.

Methods have been developed which can provide approximate dates for production of objects. The best known is radiocarbon dating, which measures the amount of naturally occurring radioactivity in organic materials. Another very valuable technique, and one frequently used for identifying fake ceramic objects, is thermoluminescence, which measures energy which starts to be trapped in the clay after the pots have been manufactured.

On occasion, Museum research scientists accompany excavations, contributing information on the ancient environment of the site and the food economy of its inhabitants.

ABOVE

*The scanning electron microscope (SEM) being used to examine a Roman silver coin.*

LEFT

*Lindow Man, discovered in a peat bog in 1978, being cleaned and investigated by a multidisciplinary team of scientists. The questions they sought to answer were many and varied, including: When and how did he die? How healthy was he? What was his last meal? The British Museum conservators also faced the difficult task of ensuring that the body would not decay and would eventually be presentable for public exhibition.*

# THE FUTURE

FOUNDED BY AN Act of Parliament in 1753, the British Museum is the earliest national museum of its kind. It is regarded by many people as the inspiration for all antiquities and history museums. In the year 2003 the Museum's 250th anniversary will be celebrated. By that time, the British Museum will be much better placed to fulfil its responsibilities for the generations to come.

The British Library separated administratively from the Museum in 1973 and its move from Bloomsbury is now complete. The Museum badly needs the space that the Library has vacated: visitor figures increased from 2.4 million in 1973 to 5.6 million in 1998 and this trend is expected to continue. An architectural brief for utilising the space and providing better facilities was drawn up

ABOVE

*Floor felt (shyrdak). Kitchi Kemin village, Chu oblast, Kyrghzstan, c. 1960. The Cloth-workers' Centre for World Textiles will open in 2000.*

in 1993. The contract was won by Sir Norman Foster and Partners, whose scheme allows for a major new Centre for Education for adults and children, new galleries for the Department of Ethnography, cloakrooms, restaurants and shops, and, above all, more space for the Museum's visitors. This huge undertaking, the Great Court, will be complete by the end of the year 2000.

The issues of storage and public access to objects not displayed have also been addressed. The Study Centre, in a building situated only one minute's walk from the front gates of the Museum, will open in 2000. There will be 'behind the scenes' visits for the public, as well as demonstrations of how archaeological material is processed. The Cloth-workers' Centre for World Textiles will be a major part of the Study

## DISPLAYS IN THE GALLERIES

For most visitors to the British Museum it is the galleries which are the primary attraction – be it the famous collection of mummies, the Parthenon sculptures or the clocks and watches room – and the Museum is deeply concerned to present its collections in the most interesting, stimulating and accessible ways possible. This is the responsibility not only of curators but also of educators and designers, who develop ideas about presentation which are both visually appealing and helpful to the public in conveying information. The lighting, backgrounds and disposition of the displays matter as much as the selection of objects and the texts describing them and their cultural or historical context.

*HSBC Money Gallery, opened January 1997.*

*The Weston Gallery of Roman Britain, opened July 1997.*

Centre, and there will be an associated conservation laboratory for organic materials. The entire reserve collections of the Prehistoric and Romano-British and the Ethnography departments, and parts of many other departments, will be housed in the Study Centre, and Student Rooms and libraries will facilitate all kinds of research on a greatly increased scale.

It is inconceivable that the work of a museum like the British Museum can ever come to an end. New kinds of objects are always being produced which throw light on the development and interaction of different cultures; there is the fundamental responsibility to record changes through the preservation of artefacts. Apart from this, the needs of the public change, and these are reflected in collecting and exhibition policies. This process has continued since the foundation of the British Museum and strains on available resources have been ever present.

In recent years the government has encouraged the Museum to meet an increasing proportion of its costs by securing charitable giving, commercial sponsorship and through trading activities. Though there might be a danger that the Museum's fundamental aims could be distorted by the relentless quest for income, the commitment to 'curious and studious persons' remains unchanged. The developments outlined above, the rolling programme of gallery renewal and an exciting and vibrant events programme are intended to maintain the British Museum's place among the top museums in the world, into the next millennium.

## INFORMATION ABOUT THE COLLECTIONS

The Museum contains in excess of six million objects, which are in the process of being recorded in a massive computer database catalogue. This provides a vital source of information about the collections to staff and visitors. In 1997 a major new interactive multimedia project, known as Compass, was initiated. This will provide a wide range of information about individual items in the collections and allow users to explore a variety of themes.

ABOVE

*A computer-generated view of the Centre for Education, which will be completed by the year 2000.*

TOP LEFT

*Computer-generated view of the east side of the Great Court showing a section of the two-acre courtyard covered by a spectacular glass roof.*

# FURTHER READING

Suggested titles are listed in the order in which the themes are covered in this book. All are published by British Museum Press.

*Treasures of the British Museum*, Marjorie Caygill, 1985, 2nd edn 1992 (0 7141 1727 7)
*The Story of the British Museum*, Marjorie Caygill, 1981, 2nd edn 1992 (0 7141 1728 5)
*The Collections of the British Museum*, Edited by David M. Wilson, 1989 (0 7141 2119 3)

*Ancient Near Eastern Art*, Dominique Collon, 1995 (0 7141 1135 X)
*Assyrian Sculpture*, Julian Reade, 1983 (0 7141 2020 0)
*Mesopotamia*, Julian Reade, 1991 (0 7141 2078 2)
*Persian Myths*, Vesta Sarkhosh Curtis, 1993 (0 7141 2082 0)

*Islamic Art*, Barbara Brend, 1991 (0 7141 1443 X)
*Islamic Tiles*, Venetia Porter, 1995 (0 7141 1456 1)

*The British Museum Book of Ancient Egypt*, Edited by Stephen Quirke and Jeffrey Spencer, 1992 (0 7141 0965 7)
*British Museum Dictionary of Ancient Egypt*, Ian Shaw and Paul Nicholson, 1995 (0 7141 0982 7)
*Egyptian Myths*, George Hart, 1990 (0 7141 2064 2)

*The British Museum Book of Chinese Art*, Edited by Jessica Rawson, 1992 (0 7141 1453 7)
*Chinese Pottery and Porcelain*, S.J.Vainker, 1995 (0 7141 1470 7)
*Hindu Art*, T. Richard Blurton, 1992 (0 7141 1442 1)

*Japanese Art: Masterpieces in the British Museum*, Lawrence Smith, Victor Harris and Timothy Clark, 1990 (0 7141 1446 4)
*Masks: The Art of Expression*, Edited by John Mack, pbk 1996 (0 7141 2530 X)

*The Art of Benin*, Paula Girshick Ben-Amos, 2nd edn 1995 (0 7141 2520 2)
*African Designs*, Rebecca Jewell, 1994 (0 7141 8074 2)
*African Textiles*, John Picton and John Mack, 1989 (0 7141 1595 9)
*Smashing Pots: Feats of Clay from Africa*, Nigel Barley, 1994 (0 7141 2513 X)

*Maori: Art and Culture*, Edited by D.C. Starzecka, 1996 (0 7141 2524 5)

*Ancient Mexico in the British Museum*, Colin McEwan, 1994 (0 7141 2516 4)
*Aztec and Maya Myths*, Karl Taube, 1993 (0 7141 1742 0)

*First Peoples, First Contacts: Native Peoples of North America*, J.C.H. King, 1999 (0 7141 2538 5)

*Britain and the Celtic Iron Age*, Simon James and Valery Rigby, 1997 (0 7141 2306 4)
*Celtic Art*, Ian Stead, 2nd edn 1997 (0 7141 2117 7)
*Celtic Myths*, Miranda J. Green, 1993 (0 7141 2091 X)

*Ancient Cyprus*, Veronica Tatton-Brown, 2nd edn 1997 (0 7141 2120 7)
*Greek Vases*, Dyfri Williams, 1999 (0 7141 2138 X)
*The Elgin Marbles*, B.F. Cook, 2nd edn 1997 (0 7141 2134 7)
*Greek Myths*, Lucilla Burn, 1990 (0 7141 2061 8)
*The British Museum Book of Greek and Roman Art*, Lucilla Burn, 1991 (0 7141 1297 6)

*Roman Myths*, Jane F. Gardner, 1993 (0 7141 1741 2)
*Romans*, Paul Roberts, 1996 (0 7141 2111 8)
*Roman Britain*, T.W. Potter, 2nd edn 1997 (0 7141 2118 5)

*The Transformation of the Roman World, AD400-900*, Edited by Leslie Webster and Michelle Brown, 1997 (0 7141 0585 6)

*The Lewis Chessmen*, Neil Stratford, 1997 (0 7141 0587 2)
*The Sutton Hoo Ship Burial*, Angela Care Evans, 3rd edn 1994 (0 7141 0575 9)
*The Medieval Garden*, Sylvia Landsberg, 1996 (0 7141 2080 4)
*Runes*, R.I. Page, 1987 (0 7141 8065 3)
*Norse Myths*, R.I. Page, 1990 (0 7141 2062 6)
*Scribes and Illuminators*, Christopher de Hamel, 1992 (0 7141 2049 9)

*Old Master Drawings from the Malcolm Collection*, Martin Royalton-Kisch, Hugo Chapman and Stephen Coppel, 1996 (0 7141 2610 1)
*Prints and Printmaking*, Antony Griffiths new edn 1996 (0 7141 2608 X)
*The Decorated Style: Architecture and Ornament 1240-1360*, Nicola Coldstream, 1994 (0 7141 1723 4)

*Towards Post-Modernism: Design since 1851*, Michael Collins, 2nd edn 1994 (0 7141 0578 3)

*The Art of the Conservator*, Edited by Andrew Oddy, 1992 (0 7141 2056 1)
*Science and The Past*, Edited by Sheridan Bowman, 1991 (0 7141 2071 5)
*Radiocarbon Dating*, Sheridan Bowman, 1990 (0 7141 2047 2)

## ACKNOWLEDGEMENTS

© 1997 The Trustees of the British Museum
Published by British Museum Press
A division of The British Museum Company Ltd
46 Bloomsbury Street, London WC1B 3QQ

First published 1997
Fourth impression 1999

British Library Cataloguing in Publication Data
A catalogue record for this book is available from the British Library
0 7141 2119 3

Compiled by R.G.W. Anderson, with special thanks to Clive Cheesman and Delia Pemberton
Designed by The Bridgewater Book Company, with special thanks to Kevin Knight and John Christopher
Internal maps by Lorraine Harrison
Cover maps by Nigel Coath for Jeffery Design
Printed in Great Britain by Butler & Tanner Ltd, Frome, Somerset

**Photographic Acknowledgements**
p.56 Picasso, *Seated Nude*, 1906-7
© Succession Picasso/DACS 1999
p.57 Laszlo Moholy-Nagy, *Construction I*, 1923
© DACS 1999
All the photographs were provided by the British Museum Photographic Service, except the following: p.2 (below left) Towneley Hall Art Gallery and Museums, Burnley Borough Council; p.5 (top) Sarah Posey; p.59 (top) Pippa Cruickshank; p.63 (left and right) and inside back cover Foster and Partners.

**Cover Illustrations**
Front cover, clockwise from top left: Medals of Mary I, AD1555, and Elizabeth I, c. AD1580-90; a knight, bishop and warder from the Lewis Chessmen, Scandinavian, mid-twelfth century AD; Dragonesque Brooch, Romano-British, c. AD100; cosmetic vessel in the form of a fish, Egyptian, eighteenth dynasty, c. 1350BC; neck-amphora, made in Campania, c. 350-325BC; head of the coffin lid of Pasenhor, Egyptian, Third Intermediate Period, c. 730-680BC; gold buckle from the Sutton Hoo ship burial, seventh century AD; turquoise mosaic serpent, Mixtec-Aztec, AD1400-1521. Front cover, flap: large stoneware lohan, Chinese, Liao dynasty, AD907-1125.